94 95 · 96   97 99   02
 7   77   11   77   111   71

ANIMAL RIGHTS

ANIMAL RIGHTS

A HANDBOOK FOR YOUNG ADULTS

BY DANIEL COHEN

THE MILLBROOK PRESS · BROOKFIELD, CT.

Photographs courtesy of Bettmann Archive: p. 13; ASPCA: p. 15;
AP/Wide World Photos: pp. 18, 46, 62; Greenpeace/Cully: p. 21;
American Humane Association: pp. 28 (Curt Ransom), 51 (Wildlife
Refuge Reform Coalition), 67 (Jennifer Orme); PETA: pp. 30, 40, 60,
79; Ginger Giles: pp. 73, 91; Cleveland Metroparks Zoo: p. 86.

Library of Congress Cataloging-in-Publication Data

Cohen, Daniel, 1936–
Animal rights: A handbook for young adults/by Daniel Cohen.
p.   cm.
Includes bibliographical references and index.
Summary: Discusses animals as a food source, as the objects of
hunting and trapping, as pets, and as the subject of the animal
rights movement.
ISBN 1-56294-219-0 (lib. bdg.)
1. Animal rights—United States—Juvenile literature.   2. Animal
rights—Juvenile literature.   [1. Animal rights.   2. Animals—
Treatment.]   I. Title.
HV4764.C58   1993
179'.3—dc20   92-40875   CIP   AC

Published by The Millbrook Press
2 Old New Milford Road, Brookfield, Connecticut 06804

CONTENTS

*To all the animals who have
shared my life and have
given me so much more than
I was ever able to give them.*

WHAT ARE ANIMAL RIGHTS?

1

The modern animal rights movement is not just about patting puppies and rescuing kittens from trees. Despite its rather benign name, animal rights is one of the most controversial topics in America today. It's tough, aggressive, and abrasive. It forces us to face a lot of uncomfortable, even horrifying truths about how our comfortable and pleasant way of life is sustained. It provides a new and radical way of looking at the world and the creatures that we share it with.

Inevitably, a fierce movement like this has stirred up fierce and often hysterical opposition. Animal rights activists have been called lunatics, irreligious subversives, dangerous radicals, and even terrorists. One antianimal rights editorial was headlined "And you thought Charles Manson was nuts."

What exactly is the animal rights movement all about? Where and how did it begin?

In order to understand what the animal rights movement is and why it is so profoundly upsetting to so many people we first have to look honestly at how we treat animals.

Of course we love our own pets, and we get all mushy over pictures of cute kittens and puppies. We want to save the whales and preserve the spotted owl. But realistically speaking the general attitude toward most animals is that they don't really matter very much. If animal suffering benefits us, and if we don't have to see the suffering, then it's okay. How many of us really care about the fate of a chicken or a white rat?

The belief in human domination over animals is deeply embedded in Western thought. At the very beginning of the Bible we read:

"Then God said, 'Let us make man in our image, after our likeness; and let them have dominion over the fish of the sea, and over the birds of the air, . . . and over all the earth, and over every creeping thing that creeps upon the earth.'

"So God created man in his own image, in the image of God he created him; male and female he created them.

"And God blessed them, and God said to them, 'Be fruitful and multiply, and fill the earth and subdue it; and have dominion over the fish of the sea and over the birds of the air and over every living thing that moves upon the earth.' "

Though it is not entirely clear, it appears as though there was no killing of animals for food or anything else in the Garden of Eden. But after Adam and Eve were expelled from the Garden the meaning of dominion became very clear. Adam and Eve were clothed in animal skins. Their son Abel kept a flock of sheep and offered some of them as sacrifices to the Lord.

When the Flood subsided, the message of dominion was repeated with renewed force and vigor.

"And God blessed Noah and his sons, and said to them, '. . . The fear of you and the dread of you shall be upon every beast of the earth, and upon every bird of the air, upon everything that creeps on the ground and all the fish of the sea; into your hand they are delivered. Every moving thing that lives shall be food for you; . . .' "

Among the ancient Greeks there was at least one school of philosophy that urged animals to be treated with respect. But the dominant view was that animals were clearly insignificant creatures, meant only for human use.

The ancient Romans would bring wild animals from throughout their far-reaching empire and put them in an arena where they would fight to the death, to the great amusement of huge crowds of Roman citizens. A widely read Roman book on agriculture said that farm animals should be treated with no more consideration than any other tool.

The Romans were consistent. They also enjoyed watching men fight to the death, and they were as indifferent to the welfare of their human slaves as they were to their animals.

Christianity incorporated ancient Hebrew as well as Greek and Roman traditions and beliefs. Many of the harsher practices were modified. For example, fights to the death between men were banned. But the attitude toward animals, as creatures meant only to serve human needs, remained

[11]

unchanged. Centuries of bullfighting, dogfighting, cockfighting, and the like indicated that Christians had not lost the old Roman habit of regarding animal suffering as a source of entertainment.

Not all animals were treated badly. A favorite horse or dog might be held in high regard by its master. The conqueror Alexander the Great had a favorite horse and when the horse died he had a city named after it. The mad Roman emperor Caligula appointed his favorite horse to the Roman Senate. Frederick the Great, the eighteenth-century king of Prussia, asked to be buried among his hunting dogs rather than his relatives, because he liked his dogs better.

More seriously, Saint Francis of Assisi preached love and respect for all living things, indeed for all nature. He is regarded as the patron saint of animals. There were some Christian sects that taught the sanctity of all life, and adopted a vegetarian lifestyle. But the overwhelming message of mainstream Western religion was one of "man's dominion."

Some philosophers even said that since animals did not possess the ability to reason they did not possess the ability to suffer. Even when animals looked as if they were suffering, that was just some sort of automatic reaction. Therefore, it didn't make any difference what was done to animals.

In the middle of the nineteenth century, Charles Darwin's theory of evolution exploded upon the Western world. Darwin said that human beings "descended," or evolved, from other animal forms. Humans, said Darwin, were animals: extremely intelligent and clever animals, but animals nonetheless. It was a direct attack on the belief that there is a

Saint Francis of Assisi (1182-1226) is the
patron saint of animals. He felt that all
animals were his brothers and sisters. The
custom of having a manger scene at Christ-
mastime was begun by Francis, which is why
the baby Christ child is usually surrounded
by common farm animals.

wall between humans and the "lower animals." Now a lot of people didn't accept Darwin's ideas, and some still don't. But Western thought had become increasingly scientific by Darwin's time, and evolution was accepted by the scientific community and rapidly became part of the general culture. Belief in evolution didn't make people suddenly rush out and embrace the horse that was pulling their carriage as a brother. But it was no longer as easy to believe that you could mistreat animals because they didn't suffer, either.

In fact, the idea that it was wrong to treat animals cruelly was making headway in England even before Darwin. Voices were raised against cruel "sports" like bullbaiting, where a specially bred dog fought a tethered bull. A small group of humanitarians got together to form the Royal Society for the Prevention of Cruelty to Animals (RSPCA). Despite ridicule and hostility from those who believed that animals were property and nothing should interfere with "property rights," the group managed to get a few modest anticruelty bills through Parliament.

Henry Bergh was a wealthy New Yorker who Abraham Lincoln had sent as a diplomat to Russia. One day Bergh came upon a man beating his horse, which had fallen from exhaustion from pulling a heavy wagon. When the man wouldn't stop, Bergh ran over and grabbed the whip from the man's hand. It was a moment that changed his life. When Bergh returned to the United States he founded the American Society for the Prevention of Cruelty to Animals (ASPCA), based on the British society. The American society officially opened in 1866, and it marks the beginning of the humane or animal welfare move-

Philanthropist Henry Bergh took a leading part in organizing the American Society for the Prevention of Cruelty to Animals.

ment in the United States. As in England there was hostility and ridicule, but the group made some headway in getting laws passed against some of the more obvious forms of cruelty. The ASPCA was also given the authority to enforce these laws.

One of the charges, then and now, that is leveled against those who have tried to make the lives of animals better is that they care only about animals and not about people. But the ASPCA led directly to the establishment of the American Society for the Prevention of Cruelty to Children, one of the first organizations in America aimed at protecting the rights of abused children. Many of those connected with the Royal Society for the Prevention of Cruelty to Animals in England had also been leaders in the fight against slavery, and many of the early feminists in America refused to eat meat. The idea that those who cared about animals didn't care about people was simply untrue.

Public opinion about animal treatment slowly began to change. It was no longer considered socially acceptable to beat a tired horse in the street or drown a litter of unwanted puppies. And you might even get in trouble with the law. Organizations like the ASPCA and various humane societies worked to get stray dogs and cats off the street and to improve conditions for laboratory animals and animals used in circuses or other performances.

Although progress was slow, by the 1960s the attitudes toward public cruelty to animals were far different than they had been in the 1860s. But out of sight of the public, some quite terrible things were happening.

In 1964 a book called *Animal Machines* by Ruth Harrison was published in England. This book exposed in gruesome detail what was happening to animals as farming changed from the old-fashioned family farm to the huge factory farm.

The book that really started the animal rights movement was *Animal Liberation*, written by an Australian professor of philosophy, Peter Singer, and published in 1975.

All of the previous humane and animal welfare groups said that we should be compassionate to animals because it was the right thing to do. But that kindness was a gift that superior humans bestowed on the "lower animals." Singer's quite novel, even revolutionary notion was that the "lower animals" had rights just like we do.

Singer took a lot of his ideas from the civil rights movement, the women's movement, and other "liberation" movements of the time. Singer argued that for centuries minority groups, women, poor people, and others had been dominated and abused by those who had the power to do so. But that didn't mean that the minorities, the women, the poor, and the others didn't have rights, even if they lacked the power to exercise them.

Animals too had rights, said Singer. They had the right not to be abused, not to be killed, and the right to live the life that they were fitted for, not just a life that served human needs and desires. Singer had another novel idea: Common and unattractive animals had as many rights as rare and interesting and cute ones. In the animal rights view an ordinary laboratory rat had as much of a right to avoid suffering and premature death as the endangered blue whale or for that matter the family dog. Just because people had the power to deny animals their rights didn't mean those rights didn't exist. To words like sexism and racism Singer added the word speciesism—the immoral belief that only human beings really matter.

Singer himself admitted that his book "may sound more like a parody of other liberation movements than a serious objective." But he was quite serious, and his work got a good deal of favorable attention. Still, the idea of animal rights seemed so far out of the mainstream of popular opinion that few thought it would catch on. Singer noted that ideas like the abolition of slavery were also once considered to be idealistic and too far-out to ever catch on. Yet even Singer himself was surprised at just how quickly his ideas did catch on. Within ten years of the publication of *Animal Liberation* there was a full-fledged animal liberation or animal rights movement in the United States and Britain.

Animal rights supporters have devised many creative ways to express their distaste for the raising and killing of animals in order to make fur coats.

Much of the groundwork for the animal rights movement had been laid by the ecology or environmental movement. Instead of furthering the domination of the human species over the environment, the ecology movement asks us to live in harmony with the natural world, and that includes the world's animals. The ecology movement had already seriously attacked the ancient view of human "dominion."

Today what can properly be called the animal rights movement is a large and extremely vocal and energetic collection of organizations and individuals. But aside from sharing a passionate belief that animals are often treated very badly, and should be treated better, these groups and individuals don't all come to the same conclusions about what should be done. There is no single animal rights "party line."

Animal rights supporters have joined (some would say infiltrated) established animal welfare and humane organizations. They have often given these organizations new life and energy. Not all of these organizations have adopted the full animal rights philosophy. For example, in the view of the animal rights purist, purebred dogs are animals created strictly to please human whims and fashions, and that is wrong. Yet the president of the ASPCA (largest of the animal welfare groups) is Roger Caras, a well-known writer on animals and the announcer at the Westminster Kennel Club dog show, America's premier showcase for purebred dogs.

At the other end of the spectrum is the radical People for the Ethical Treatment of Animals (PETA—pronounced PETE-a). This relatively new but very active and growing group espouses, among other things, total vegetarianism and the abolition of all laboratory tests on animals. PETA tactics have included boycotts, picketing, and direct confrontation with those they consider exploiters of animals, such as hunters or people who buy fur coats.

And there are those underground groups that engage in even more militant and often illegal direct action. Animal rights supporters have broken into laboratories in order to find what they believe to be evidence of abuse and to "liberate" some laboratory animals. There have even been a few (very few) attempted bombings.

The effectiveness of a movement can often be measured by the depth of the anger of those who oppose it. If this is true of the animal rights movement, then they have been very effective indeed, for their opponents, and they range from scientists who use laboratory animals to hunters to dog breeders, have been quite frenzied. The growth of the animal rights movement has been compared to the growth of the Nazi party in Germany, and animal rights activists have been labeled terrorists who have modeled themselves on underground groups like the Irish Republican Army. In fact, many of the tactics of animal rights groups are patterned on the very successful activities of environmental groups like Greenpeace, which have, among other things, confronted whaling ships and seal hunters, to stop them and get maximum publicity for the environmental message. Greenpeace activists have also been labeled lunatics and terrorists by their opponents. Today, however, Greenpeace is widely admired, even by people who don't agree with everything they do.

As a Japanese whaling fleet factory ship hauls a whale aboard in the Southern Ocean off Antarctica, Greenpeace representatives protest from their inflatable boat.

Animal rights can no longer be considered a "fringe" topic. Whether we like them or not, the ideas and actions of the animal rights supporters intrude on our daily lives. They may influence what we eat, what we wear, and how we think about the world and our relationship to other living things.

In the following chapters we are going to look at how these ideas and activities have affected a wide variety of areas, from agriculture to zoos. The facts that must be presented are often unpleasant at best, and the questions raised do not have easy answers. Sometimes they have no answers at all. But animal rights is a subject that should not, and really can not, be avoided in our society.

THE UNHAPPY HEN

2

When you bite into a hamburger or devour a plate of spicy Buffalo "wings," you are certainly aware, in a general sort of way, that you are eating the flesh of a once living animal. But that is not usually the sort of subject that dominates your lunch or dinner conversation. Nor are you likely to think very much about how the animal that you are now eating lived and died. For most of us our meat comes already cooked, or it is purchased from the supermarket in a neat plastic tray. There is virtually no blood, and the cut-up pieces of cow or chicken seem as disconnected from real animals as a block of tofu.

But these are the very subjects that supporters of animal rights think about a lot. In fact, how we obtain our food is probably the single most important topic on the animal rights agenda.

Animal rights philosopher Peter Singer says:

"The use and abuse of animals raised for food far exceeds, in sheer numbers of animals affected, any other kinds of mistreatment. Over 100 million cows, pigs, and sheep are raised and slaughtered in the United States alone each year; and for poultry the figure is a staggering five billion . . . It is here, on our dinner table and in our neighborhood supermarket or butcher's shop, that we are brought into direct touch with the most extensive exploitation of other species that has ever existed."

There has been a good deal of argument over whether we are "natural" meat eaters or vegetarians. Were our prehuman ancestors peaceful plant eaters or aggressive carnivorous apes? In nature the line between plant eater and meat eater is not always a well-defined one. A grizzly bear will gorge itself on blueberries, fish, and young deer. The bulk of a wild chimpanzee's diet is plant matter, but it will also eat insects and on occasion hunt, kill, and eat small animals.

Of all the creatures on Earth, human beings appear to have the most varied diet. It ranges from many of the people of India who, for religious and economic reasons, are strict vegetarians to the Eskimos, who eat only meat and fish, because vegetables don't grow in the Arctic. We human beings are a highly opportunistic species. We eat whatever is available.

Today the vast majority of Americans live in cities and suburbs, and have never even seen a farm—not a real modern farm anyway. We have sort of a vague idea of what a farm is supposed to look like; an idea that comes from storybooks and old movies. There is a neat red barn with a couple of cows and pigs. During the day the cows graze in green fields, while the pigs wallow in a mud bath. A small flock of chickens, presided over by a haughty rooster, wanders about the barnyard scratching up grain. Occasionally a few of these animals might be killed to feed the farmer and his family or perhaps to provide food for families in the distant city. They die humanely, after living a full and fairly free life.

This idyllic picture was always mostly fantasy anyway. Life on the farm was tough, and good old Farmer Brown was not at all sentimental about the animals he raised for food. Today the red barn, the grazing cows, and scratching chickens are about as far removed from the realities of modern farming as Disney's Magic Kingdom is from the worst ghetto that you can imagine.

It is impossible to have millions of cows, pigs, and sheep and billions of chickens living on small farms. Over the last fifty years or so, American farming has changed. The small family-run farm has almost disappeared. It has been replaced by huge mechanized farms, often owned by giant corporations. Farming has become the agribusiness, and modern farms are often referred to, quite accurately, as factory farms. This change has not only affected wheat, corn, and soybeans but farm animals as well. Nowhere is this more obvious than in the way chickens are now raised.

Not so very long ago chicken was not an everyday part of the American diet. Often it was a special treat—a roasted chicken for Sunday dinner. Today chicken is the meat of choice for many people. It is supposed to be healthier than "red meat," and it is relatively cheap. But the agribusiness could never meet the American appetite for chicken if they were still raised in the old-fashioned way.

Today chickens do not run about the barnyard. They are raised indoors in huge windowless sheds. The sheds contain anywhere from 10,000 to 50,000 chickens each. These "broilers," as chickens destined for eating are called, are placed inside the sheds when they are a day or two old. Their environment is completely regulated with the aim of producing the largest chicken in the shortest time at the lowest cost.

Food and water are delivered automatically from bins and tanks. Lighting is controlled. At first lights may be kept on twenty-four hours a day, because that encourages the chickens to eat and thus gain weight more quickly. Later lighting is reduced until finally the shed is kept in a state of semidarkness all the time.

Chicken producers (one can hardly call them farmers) believe that low light reduces aggression. The huge cramped flocks are so unnatural that once chickens begin to grow, they also begin to fight with one another. This "vice," as chicken producers call it, results in mutilation and death, but most significantly it results in unsalable birds. The best way to keep chickens from fighting would be to reduce the overcrowding, but this would also make the production of chickens more expensive.

A radical solution to fighting that is now employed by many chicken producers is called "debeaking." It's exactly what it sounds like. The chicken's upper beak is cut off. Chicken producers don't like to talk about debeaking, but when they do, they say it is a painless process, like cutting one's fingernails. It isn't.

Despite ventilation, the air inside a poultry shed is filled with dust and smells awful. These confined and overcrowded birds suffer from a variety of diseases and their behavior has been completely distorted. It would not be an exaggeration to say that the conditions they live in drive them crazy. Sometimes a loud noise or other disturbance will panic the birds. They will all rush to one corner, piling on top of one another. Those at the bottom smother. Mortality is high, but these broiler sheds are still more "cost effective" than raising birds under more humane conditions.

At the age of about seven or eight weeks the broilers are considered large enough for slaughter. Under normal conditions a chicken will live about seven years. The chickens are crammed into crates, loaded onto trucks, and shipped off to the processing plants.

Perhaps while driving along the highway you have passed one of these trucks loaded with crates of live chickens. The trucks are trailed by a cloud of feathers, and if you get close enough the smell is terrible. It is the sort of sight that makes you automatically look away.

At the processing plant the crates are unloaded. After a wait that can be several hours, the chickens are hauled out of the crates, hung up by one leg on a conveyor belt and have their throats cut. It is the not-very-merciful end of a short and miserable existence.

And if you think that's bad, the factory farms that produce eggs are even worse. Newly hatched chicks are sorted out. Males, since they don't lay eggs, are discarded—literally thrown away. They are either gassed or dumped alive into plastic containers, where they suffocate. The females are placed in tiers of cramped wire cages called "batteries," where they

Egg-layers are often raised in wire cages that allow their eggs to roll down to a conveyor belt. On a highly automated egg farm, one worker can care for as many as 100,000 laying hens.

spend the rest of their lives. They barely have enough space to turn around, and often their toenails grow around the wire on the bottom of their cages, so they can't move at all. The sights, sounds, and smells inside these egg factories are hellish. As in the broiler sheds, mortality rates run high. Four or five chickens crammed into a tiny cage together may actually begin to cannibalize one another unless they are debeaked, which they are. But when examining the bottom line, egg producers have determined that this is the most profitable way of producing their product.

Hens continue to lay eggs profitably until they are about a year old. By that time their bodies are simply exhausted. They are then slaughtered and sold as chicken parts or soup chickens.

What happens to chickens represents the most extreme form of factory farming. But to a greater or lesser degree almost all animals raised for food—turkeys, pigs, cows, sheep—are subjected to the unnatural assembly-line conditions of the factory farm. Pigs, probably the most intelligent of farm animals, spend their entire short lives in small concrete stalls, where they have nothing to do but eat, sleep, and gain weight. The fact that they go nearly mad from crowding and boredom (many have their teeth "clipped" to keep them from biting themselves) does not figure into the profit calculations of the factory farmer one bit. At the age of about six months the pigs are slaughtered.

Animal rights groups have singled out the fate of "veal calves" as being particularly cruel. At the age of a day or two the calves are taken from their mothers and confined in pens so small that they

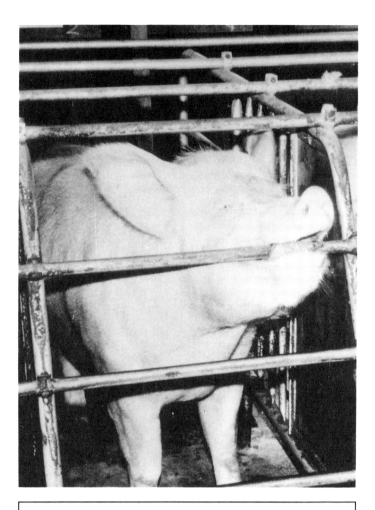

Hogs are valued as a source of pork chops, bacon, ham, and sausage. On factory farms these intelligent animals are raised in confined conditions that give them virtually no chance to exercise.

cannot even turn around. They are kept on an unnatural and unhealthy diet of milky gruel, which produces the light-colored flesh that people seem to prefer. That's what "milk-fed" veal means. Under these conditions most veal calves get sick, and are fed large quantities of drugs, just so that they can be kept alive and growing for sixteen weeks or so. Then the calves, often too sick and crippled to walk, are taken out of their pens and killed.

It would be easy to go on and on, piling one gruesome detail upon another. But you get the picture of life and death down on the factory farm. It is a business run strictly for profit. The living animals are given no more consideration than the metal and plastic parts of an automobile on an assembly line.

Agribusiness public relations spokesmen say that if the animals were not healthy and happy they would not grow and reproduce. The claim is nonsense. Many of the animals are kept alive and growing, at least for the brief time they are allowed to live, with massive doses of drugs and hormones. Factory farmers are obsessive about keeping visitors and cameras out of their sheds, barns, and slaughterhouses. You will see lots of pictures of fields of waving wheat but very few of battery hens or veal calves. It is a business that is conducted strictly behind closed doors.

In Europe, particularly in the Scandinavian countries like Sweden, governments have passed some legislation curbing the worst excesses of factory farming. The movement in Sweden was led by Astrid Lindgren, creator of the popular children's book character Pippi Longstocking. In the United States there are virtually no regulations and very little chance that there will be any soon. The agribusiness is big and powerful. It is the second-largest industry in the United States. Regulations, we are told, interfere with "market forces" and "free enterprise." Besides, would you be willing to pay more for your hamburger or Buffalo wings?

For the committed believer in animal rights the only course of action is to become a vegetarian. "Love animals—don't eat them" is a popular motto. Ethical vegetarianism—that is, refusal to eat meat because of the belief that it is wrong to kill animals for food—has been around for a long time. Most Hindus refuse to eat meat for religious reasons. For well over a century there have been vegetarian societies in England and the United States. There was even a small vegetarian political party. But it was the growth of factory farming and all its attendant horrors that really inspired the growth of vegetarianism in the West. In fact it was a reaction to factory farming, more than anything else, that fueled the growth of the whole animal rights movement.

There are several kinds of vegetarians. There are *total vegetarians*, who eat no animal foods, eggs, or dairy products. Remember those egg factories. *Vegans* go even further; they don't use any products derived from animals, including wool. *Lacto-vegetarians* include milk and cheese in their diets and *lacto-ovo-vegetarians* eat eggs as well. *Pesco-vegetarians* will eat fish, and *pollo-vegetarians* will eat poultry but no "red meat."

And there are many who are sympathetic to the vegetarian idea, but can't quite make the full commitment. They try to avoid eating meat as often as possible. Many people won't eat veal, because of the cruelty involved in its production.

[32]

In some places it is possible to buy what are called "free-range" meats; that is, meat from animals that were not raised under factory farm conditions. It is also possible to get "organic" eggs, which were laid by chickens that do not spend their lives in cages. Free-range meats and organic eggs are not all that easy to find, except in certain health food stores or in college towns or other areas that have a large number of people interested in animal rights or environmental issues. But free-range meat is also supposed to contain less fat and thus be healthier, and it is becoming more widely available.

Vegetarians have a whole list of reasons why their diet is better for the animals, for you, and for the environment. The cholesterol found in animal fat has been linked to heart disease and cancer. If you don't eat meat or eggs you are not exposed to all the hormones, antibiotics, and other drugs that are fed to animals on factory farms. Pesticides that are used on plants tend to concentrate in the flesh of the plant-eating animals that human beings eat. Statistics seem to indicate that vegetarians actually do live longer and are generally healthier than people who eat lots of meat. Even the U.S. government has finally suggested that people cut down on the consumption of meat and dairy products, for health reasons. This suggestion was made over the strong objections of the powerful meat and dairy lobbies.

Meat producers have countered with ad campaigns hinting that if you don't eat meat you are some kind of a weakling or sissy. "Real beef for real people" was one of the slogans. Of course, the soldiers of the ancient Roman army, perhaps the toughest and most efficient fighting force the world has ever known, lived almost exclusively on a diet of cereals. Roman soldiers would only eat meat when there was no cereal. It was the weak and decadent aristocrats of Rome who were the meat eaters.

At one time it was believed that athletes had to eat lots of meat protein before a big game or a big race. Today most marathon runners, who are probably the best-conditioned athletes in the world, load up on pasta, not steak, before a race.

Vegetarians also regularly trot out statistics indicating that meat production, particularly factory farming, is both inefficient and harmful to the environment.

Here are just a few examples:

Forests throughout the world are being destroyed to make room for cattle grazing. The destruction of rain forests in Central and South America have been particularly severe. Much of the beef that winds up in fast-food hamburgers comes from cattle grazed on what used to be a tropical rain forest.

Parts of the United States are chronically short of water, and the problem is only going to get worse. It takes some 2,500 gallons (9,450 liters) of fresh water to produce a single pound (about half a kilogram) of beef. In addition, livestock manure may be the greatest source of water pollution in the United States.

It takes 16 pounds (7 kilograms) of grain to produce a pound (about half a kilogram) of beef. If all Americans became vegetarians there would be enough grain left over to feed all the starving people in the world.

One acre (about half a hectare) of pasture produces 165 pounds (75 kilograms) of beef. The same acre can produce 20,000 pounds (9,080 kilograms) of potatoes.

The details of these statistics can be argued with. But no one can seriously argue with the conclusion that in a world that is increasingly short of resources, meat production is not the most efficient way to produce food. That's why really poor people in most parts of the world are vegetarians.

The popularity of vegetarianism has grown dramatically in the United States. Today there are some 15 million vegetarians—about twice as many as there were just ten years ago. How many of these people are ethical vegetarians and how many have switched to meatless diets for health reasons is impossible to calculate.

It's certainly easier to be a vegetarian today than it once was. You don't have to limit yourself to a diet of beans and brown rice. There are now lots of vegetarian restaurants and practically every good restaurant has at least a couple of vegetarian dishes on the menu. Even some hamburger-based fast-food restaurants now offer salads, baked potatoes, or other vegetarian alternatives. And, of course, pizza has become the food of choice for teen vegetarians. Supermarkets, and particularly health food stores, offer a variety of vegetarian products from meatless sausages to artificial eggs and nondairy milk substitutes. Even school lunchrooms now regularly offer vegetarian dishes. There are loads of excellent vegetarian cookbooks available.

A lot of celebrities from Madonna to Leonard Nimoy, *Star Trek's* Mr. Spock, are well-known vegetarians. In fact, a vegetarian diet has become quite fashionable in some circles. At least you will not automatically be labeled a freak if you tell your friends you don't eat meat.

For the deeply committed animal rights supporter all of the arguments about health and saving the environment are nice, but quite beside the point. Vegetarianism is at the core of their beliefs. They won't eat meat because they don't want animals to suffer and die just to provide them with a meal, when other forms of food are readily available.

But many also realize that we are a meat-eating society, and eating habits are hard to change. You can start by simply cutting down on the amount of meat you eat. "You don't have to be a purist to help animals," says *The Animal Rights Handbook*.

THE BLIND RABBIT

3

In 1988 a woman named Fran Trutt, a well-known animal rights activist, was arrested while planting a bomb outside the offices of the U.S. Surgical Corporation, a medical supply company that had been using live dogs to demonstrate its surgical stapling devices. The company had long been severely criticized by animal rights activists for killing dogs as part of their "sales pitch."

The animal rights movement has often been charged by its enemies with engaging in "terrorist" activities. This is one of the few incidents in the United States in which such a charge is really justified. Even here Trutt was working alone and her action was quickly denounced by leaders of the movement. Indeed, it appears as though she was encouraged by agents from the medical supply company, as a way of discrediting animal rights activities. An informant working for U.S. Surgical actually drove her to the company offices where the bomb was to be planted. In a plea bargain, she was given a year in jail and three years probation.

Although this seems to be an isolated (but well-publicized) attempt, animal rights supporters have taken part in a lot of other activity, which was confrontational or downright illegal, against institutions that use animals in testing. Laboratories have been broken into and laboratory animals "liberated." Some institutions have also been vandalized. Animal rights leaders have openly encouraged certain types of illegal activity. Animal liberation philosopher Peter Singer speaks admiringly about a raid on a laboratory at the University of Pennsylvania where "stolen videotapes provided the evidence that finally convinced even the secretary for health and human services that the experiments must stop. It is hard to imagine that this result could have been achieved in any other way, and I have nothing but praise for the courageous, caring and thoughtful people who planned and carried out that particular action." There can be no doubt where he stands.

In Britain, militant animal liberationists have a record of greater and more indiscriminate violence than their U.S. counterparts. In 1983 an underground animal liberation group mailed letter bombs to Prime Minister Margaret Thatcher and three members of her Cabinet. One exploded and injured an office worker.

Using animals in experiments is the subject in the field of animal rights that inspires the deepest passions. And for good reason. This area seems to pit human welfare and even human life against horrible suffering and death for millions of nonhuman animals.

Those who support animal testing put the question very starkly. Animal tests, they say, result in life-saving medicines and treatments for human beings. If animal testing were abolished the quality of medical research would deteriorate dramatically and as a result many sick people would die.

The response of Tom Regan, one of the chief philosophers of the animal rights movement is unequivocal: "Those who accept the rights view, and sign for animals, will not be satisfied with anything less than the total abolition of the harmful use of animals in science—in education, in toxicity testing, in basic research."

Lest animal rights advocates be accused of favoring the lives of nonhuman animals over those of human animals (a charge that is often made) Regan is quick to point out that the rights view "plays no favorites" and that no practice that violates "human rights" is acceptable. By that he means it is also unacceptable to experiment on people who don't know or don't understand what is being done to them.

But many, perhaps the majority, of those who are sympathetic to animal rights would not go as far as Regan and demand the total abolition of the use of animals in research. Others sidestep or avoid the issue. They contend that an enormous number of animals in scientific research suffer and die in experiments that are quite unnecessary to the preservation of human welfare.

Is animal testing necessary in developing cosmetics? Cosmetics are certainly not a matter of human life and death. One of the most notorious animal tests is called the Draize Eye Irritancy Test. It

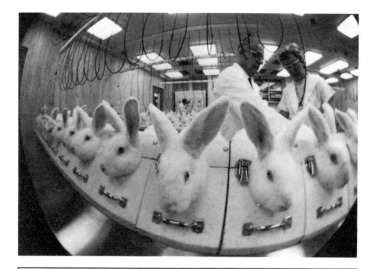

Many rabbits used in the Draize eye-irritancy test are immobilized in restraining devices from which only their heads protrude. The substance being tested is dripped into their eyes, often causing the animals to break bones in an attempt to escape.

has been used in the cosmetics industry and with a variety of household products, everything from oven cleaner to dishwashing liquid, since the 1940s. The solution being tested is poured into the eyes of conscious rabbits who have been immobilized in stocks. Sometimes the animal's eyes are held open by metal clips. Rabbits have been known to break their necks or backs in an attempt to get away from the pain during the tests. The rabbits are then observed for a week or two to see how much damage has been done to their eyes. Reactions range from irritation to ulcerations, bleeding, and blindness. No painkillers are given because these are said to "interfere" with the test. When the test is over the rabbits are killed.

The test sounds horrible, and it is. Yet the companies that used it insisted that it was "necessary" for product safety. The test, however, was not required by law. Since the 1940s other tests have been developed that do not require the hideous deaths of large numbers of rabbits. Manufacturers continued to use this cruel and outdated test mainly because lawyers told them if they ever were sued by someone who claimed to have been injured by the product, they could say that they had performed every possible safety test on it. The Draize test was really used to protect the manufacturer, not to protect the public.

In 1980 the Draize test became a primary target for the new animal rights movement. One group took out a full-page ad in *The New York Times*. It featured a picture of a rabbit with bandaged eyes confined in the stocks used for the test. It asked the question: "How many rabbits does Revlon blind for beauty's sake?" Demonstrators dressed in bunny costumes paraded in front of Revlon's corporate headquarters. The campaign got an enormous amount of publicity, and the giant cosmetics corporation began to squirm.

Eventually Revlon offered Rockefeller University, in New York City, a $1.25 million grant to find alternatives to the test. Other cosmetics companies also joined the search for alternatives.

In the late 1970s a small British company, called The Body Shop, dedicated to selling what they called cruelty-free cosmetics and body care products, began in a storefront in London. No animal tests had been used to develop any of the company's products. As the campaign against animal testing of cosmetics gathered momentum The Body Shop prospered. Sometimes their products cost a little more than the standard brands, but lots of people were willing to pay extra. Today The Body Shop is a multimillion-dollar worldwide business. Lots of other small companies have begun to produce cosmetics and household products that do not employ animal testing. Brands such as Tom's of Maine toothpaste and Bon Ami cleanser advertise the fact that they do not use animal testing in product development. Animal rights groups have actively promoted those products that don't use animal testing and loudly condemned those that do. Even the giant corporations have tried to phase out their animal testing. As soon as they began losing business the corporations discovered that those tests weren't *really* necessary after all.

The campaigns against the Draize test and the use of animals in testing cosmetics were major early successes of the animal rights movement.

In addition to the campaign against the Draize test, animal rights groups have singled out a number of other specific animal experiments as targets of criticism and action. These are generally in areas that might be considered medically nonessential or appear to be unusually cruel and painful. Campaigns have been mounted against the use of animals in psychological or behavioral tests, which include, for example, planting electrodes in the brains of monkeys and cats to see if certain signals can trigger specific types of behavior.

Government-supported tests are another frequent target because the work is supported by taxpayers' money and political pressure can be mobilized. The U.S. Navy's experimental use of dolphins to detect and clear mines was a practice widely publicized and widely condemned. Another U.S. government experiment that received a great deal of negative publicity was the use of dogs in "wound labs." Dogs were suspended from slings and shot with high-powered weapons to cause battlelike injuries for use in military surgical practice. Dolphins and dogs are, of course, very popular with the public. The use of animals in experiments to develop cancer or AIDS drugs, while deplored by many animal rights leaders, have not been highlighted by them.

Dissecting animals, usually rats or frogs, in school biology classes is another activity that has come under fire from animal rights groups. They insist that the average student learns just as much or more from a model of a frog or rat as from cutting up the real thing. Many, many individual students have objected to dissection as part of their schoolwork. At one time it might have been difficult to get out of a dissection project without some sort of penalty. Now it is a common practice to assign objecting students to alternative work. In fact, dissection in high school science laboratories appears to be on the way out. California has passed a law allowing students the right to refuse to dissect animals. At least one major textbook publisher no longer includes dissection in its popular biology text.

There have also been strong objections raised to the use of experimental animals in school science fair projects.

Campaigns against animal experimentation are not new. During the nineteenth century a large number of antivivisection societies were formed in Britain and the United States. Vivisection is the practice of performing experiments on live animals.

A less absolute position has been taken by animal welfare groups. They did not oppose all animal experimentation, but they wanted to make sure that animals used in experiments were treated as humanely as possible; that they were well cared for in the laboratory and protected from as much suffering as possible. At best, the life of a laboratory animal is a pretty dreadful one. But it can be improved by regulations. Over the years there have been a variety of laws passed that regulate the use of animals in laboratories. The most effective has been the Animal Welfare Act, passed by Congress in 1966, and amended several times since.

The problem has always been the enforcement of the animal welfare regulations. Enforcement is usually weak and often barely exists at all. People who work in laboratories are not sadists who deliberately torture animals for their own amusement. But, by and large, they regard the rats, cats, and dogs they use not so much as living things but as tools that help them in their work. They tend to look upon any regulations as an unwarranted and unnecessary intrusion into their work.

In 1979 a well-known documentary filmmaker, Joseph Weisman, filmed a documentary at the Yerkes Primate Laboratory, one of the nation's leading institutions for the study of apes and monkeys. When the documentary came out people who saw it were horrified and sickened by the scenes of the tremendous suffering of the animals, and the almost callous indifference of the researchers to the suffering. The

Yerkes staff, stung by the criticism, defended themselves by saying that the film presented only a partial and distorted picture. But, in fact, the film was accurate, and what is even more disturbing is that Yerkes was one of the best-run laboratories. Nothing shown in the film was illegal, or considered unusual or excessively cruel by the research community. If Weisman had set out to simply give animal research a bad name he could have chosen far worse places and presented more shocking scenes.

There is no way around the fact that animal experimentation, even when carried out for the best of motives by the best of researchers, inflicts terrible pain and suffering on the experimental animals. This is something that those who support animal experiments don't want the public to see. They prefer to do their work without any public interference and out of the public view. They just don't want to talk about what it is that they do, and insist the public "does not understand," and is too easily swayed by "emotional" appeals.

But animal rights activists present some convincing arguments. They insist that many animal experiments are unnecessary and repetitive, which is true. They point out that most of the improvements in human health in modern times is due to better nutrition and sanitation, rather than through medicines and techniques developed with animal subjects. That is also true. They say that medical advances like the development of penicillin and the yellow fever vaccine were made without animals. True again.

On the other hand, however, animal rights activists avoid some very important issues. For instance,

Opponents to animal research hold a rally during World Week for Laboratory Animals. There has long been debate between the medical community and animal activists as to what research, if any, is appropriate to carry out on animals in order to save humans.

they do not discuss the fact that insulin, which has saved the life of countless diabetics, was discovered through a series of experiments on dogs that inflicted enormous pain and suffering. (There were many other genuinely lifesaving drugs and treatments developed and tested through experiments in which millions upon millions of animals suffered painful deaths.) There is, at present, no adequate scientific alternative for animal experimentation in many areas.

For Ingrid Newkirk, one of the founders of the radical animal rights group PETA, there is no dilemma. She has said that even if animal tests produced a cure for AIDS, "we'd be against it."

That is probably not a sentiment that the majority of people, or even the majority of those who consider themselves supporters of animal rights, would agree with. So when Newkirk wrote a popular children's book on animal rights she talked about classroom dissection, cosmetics research, and lots of other topics. But she never mentioned AIDS research.

As in so many other areas the philosophy of animal rights presents us with tough, almost impossible choices.

KILLING FOR FUN

4.

During the nineteenth century, hunters in what was still called "the Wild West" decimated the huge herds of American bison, or buffalo. The animal that was once the symbol of the American West was brought to the verge of extinction by hunters. The passenger pigeon, once the most numerous bird in North America, actually was hunted to extinction.

Today hunting does not seriously threaten most endangered species in North America. There is the occasional rich "sportsman" who will pay a great deal of money for the chance to shoot a polar bear from an airplane. There are those who get some perverse pleasure out of shooting bald eagles. But such people are breaking the law—they are criminals.

Most ordinary hunters would never approve of this sort of activity. They would insist that they are "law-abiding citizens." Anyone who has ever lived in a hunting area knows that a great deal of law breaking goes on in the woods. Deer are hunted from the road, or illegally at night with lights, or out of season. Areas posted to prevent hunting are routinely violated. Food is spread to attract migratory ducks into range of a hunter's gun—also an illegal practice. There are hundreds of violations that regularly take place among hunters who seriously consider themselves to be law abiding. But it is the destruction of habitat, not the guns of hunters, even those who hunt illegally, that is the real threat to endangered species in the United States.

Hunters say that their activity gives them a chance to get out in the woods and enjoy nature, and to share the camaraderie of their friends. Of course, hiking, birdwatching, or nature photography could provide the same results. Hunters also insist that what they do is a "sport." That implies some sort of equal competition. The competition between a man with a high-powered rifle and a deer is hardly equal. If the man loses he goes home; if the deer loses it's dead. Hunters also say that what they are doing is okay because they eat what they kill, just like a lion or a wolf. In fact, most hunting in America is trophy hunting. The hunters are not looking for a meal. They are looking for something to stuff and hang on a wall. What with equipment, license fees, and travel costs, hunting is expensive. If all the costs were added up and then divided per pound for the amount of meat obtained, it would be far, far more than the average hunter would ever be willing to pay at the supermarket. Almost no one in America needs to "hunt to eat."

There is, of course, the usual appeal to "tradition." "My daddy hunted, his daddy before him hunted. . . ." That sort of appeal carries no more moral weight than all the other appeals to cruel traditions. After all, great-grandfather might have been a slave owner. That doesn't make slave owning a good idea today.

Hunters are on firmer ground when they argue that they have contributed a lot to wildlife conservation. Hunters have used their considerable political clout to ensure the preservation of large tracts of wildlife habitat. Private hunting and fishing clubs also keep forests and streams from being developed and polluted. A good portion of the money paid out in hunting and fishing licenses is used for wildlife maintenance and preservation. At one time hunters were not only the best, but practically the only, real conservationists in America.

But that's not true anymore. Today less than ten percent of Americans hunt. Nonhunting conservationists and ecologists are more numerous, more active, and more effective. They have become the leaders in preserving the environment.

Finally, hunters say that they fulfill an important role in nature. By killing off a certain number of deer, or rabbits, or ducks they keep the species from becoming too numerous, thereby protecting them from the horrors of starvation. Hunters see themselves taking the place of now vanished predators like wolves and mountain lions. It is far more humane, the hunters say, to be killed instantly by a clean shot from a rifle than to die slowly from starvation or to be attacked and torn to bits by a pack of wolves.

The most-hunted animal in America is undoubtedly the white-tailed deer. While the population of most large nondomestic mammals in North America

While some would consider this scene a triumphant and successful finish to a hard day of hunting, others would consider the hunter a murderer of a fellow creature.

has declined dramatically, the deer have prospered. Despite expanding suburbs and shrinking forests there are more white-tailed deer in America now than there were when the Europeans first arrived five centuries ago. They are so numerous that many suburban homeowners consider them pests who devour ornamental shrubs and trees. Whenever a bear attacks a camper, that's big news. But many more people are injured and killed when the autos in which they are riding hit or try to avoid a deer running across the road. The type of ticks that infest deer carry Lyme disease, a serious infection in humans and some domestic animals. For these reasons the deer is often regarded as the most dangerous wild animal in America.

While hunters do kill off a large number of deer every year, they are also really responsible for the great population explosion among white-tailed deer. The deer has been a favored species because it has been a favorite of hunters. Deer habitats have been protected, deer predators have been eliminated, and very often during winter when food is scarce, deer are saved from starvation by hunters who feed them. Rather than being a truly "wild" animal, the white-tailed deer is more of a semidomestic animal that is raised for the pleasure of the hunters.

Since deer hunting is primarily trophy hunting the main targets are the large bucks, the ones with the big antlers. In nature it is the large and vigorous bucks who would be the most likely to survive hunger, disease, and predators, and pass their genes on to future generations. By regularly killing off these prime specimens hunting may produce a genetically weaker strain of deer.

The hunter's comforting assumption that a bullet provides a relatively quick and clean death is a questionable one. All hunters are not perfect shots. Many deer are wounded rather than killed outright, and death may come slowly and painfully. Bow hunting is even worse. Those hunters who use a bow and arrow claim that they are more "sportsmanlike." In a sense that is true, for it is far harder to kill a deer with a bow and arrow than it is with a rifle. But bow hunters are also far more likely to wound rather than kill cleanly.

Hordes of armed men tramping through the woods every fall undoubtedly create panic among deer—hardly a kindness. Panicky deer are more likely to run out onto the road and in front of a car. The frightened deer move around a great deal at a time of year when they should be storing fat and energy for the winter. Hunting may thus contribute to starvation.

In the animal rights philosophy all of the arguments pro and con about hunting are rendered unimportant before a single and undeniable fact. The reason people hunt is not to be out in the woods, or to restore the balance of nature, or even to feed themselves. It is to kill an animal for "sport" or more bluntly for the fun of it. Hunting is a particularly obvious way of expressing the belief that nonhuman animals have no right to exist other than to serve the needs and even the whims of man, no matter how frivolous they may be. And that, say the animal rights advocates, is totally unacceptable.

In England the campaign against hunting is older and more well organized than in the United States. A particular target has been fox hunting. This is an old and colorful practice with mounted riders wearing scarlet coats, galloping across picturesque fields, followed by packs of hounds, and accompanied by the sound of horns. Paintings of fox hunting scenes adorn walls throughout England, and are popular in the United States as well. While the pictures show the beauty of the hunt, they do not show its cruelty. The fox is pursued to the point of exhaustion and then captured and often torn to bits by the dogs.

At one time when the fox represented a threat to chickens, ducks, and other livestock, there might have been some economic reason for this sort of fox hunting. But the fox is no threat anymore and hasn't been for a long time. The hunt is strictly for show. There is also a great deal of snobbery in fox hunting, for only the wealthy and well connected are ever able to take part in this "sport."

People have opposed fox hunting, not only because it is cruel, which it is, but because it was a symbol of the English class system. Rich people were able to do things that poor folk could not.

Bills to ban fox hunting have been proposed in Parliament for years. They never pass. Hunts have also been picketed for a long time. But the animal liberation movement spawned a new and more radical breed of protesters called The Hunt Saboteur Association. They don't just have picket signs. "Hunt sabs" show up at hunts and blow horns to confuse the hounds. Or they sneak into an area in the middle of the night and lay a false trail or simply make enough noise to chase any foxes well out of the way. Hunt saboteurs try to avoid violence, but confrontations between the protesters and angry fox hunters have become increasingly common and are now almost a regular feature of fox hunting in England.

Journalist and antihunt activist Philip Windeatt says that the main reason people become hunt saboteurs is because of frustration:

"Going out on a hunt sab, you really think you are doing something. It is your chance to get out there and actually stop it physically. The Hunt Saboteur Association is also a breeding ground and starting point for animal rights."

Even those who do not share the animal rights view on all hunting are horrified by the existence of what are called "hunting ranches." These ranches, which are mostly in the American Southwest, are places where a hunter with enough cash in his pocket can kill an exotic animal for a fee. For example, one of these ranches was charging $1,500 to kill a sika deer from Japan or $2,500 for an oryx from Africa. This particular ranch advertised a "No Kill No Pay Guarantee."

These ranches strip away the last shred of the argument that this sort of hunting is a "sport." The animals are almost always captive bred. They are quite unaccustomed to the area in which they are released and have no chance at all to get away from even the most inept hunters. The business is, after all, "No Kill No Pay." It is just about the same as shooting an animal in a cage. In fact, animal rights activists have videotapes showing that sometimes animals actually are shot in cages on these ranches.

Where do the animals on the hunting ranches come from? Many are raised on game "farms." And some are "surplus" animals from circuses and zoos.

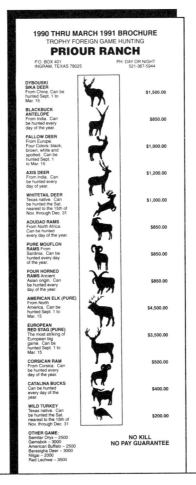

1990 THRU MARCH 1991 BROCHURE
TROPHY FOREIGN GAME HUNTING

PRIOUR RANCH

P.O. BOX 401
INGRAM, TEXAS 78025

PH: DAY OR NIGHT
521-367-5944

DYBOUSKI SIKA DEER
From China. Can be hunted Sept. 1 to Mar. 15 — $1,500.00

BLACKBUCK ANTELOPE
From India. Can be hunted every day of the year. — $850.00

FALLOW DEER
From Europe. Four Colors: black, brown, white and spotted. Can be hunted Sept. 1 to Mar. 15 — $1,000.00

AXIS DEER
From India. Can be hunted every day of year. — $1,200.00

WHITETAIL DEER
Texas native. Can be hunted the Sat. nearest to the 15th of Nov. through Dec. 31 — $1,000.00

AOUDAD RAMS
From North Africa. Can be hunted every day of the year. — $850.00

PURE MOUFLON RAMS From Sardinia. Can be hunted every day of the year. — $850.00

FOUR HORNED RAMS Ancient Asian origin. Can be hunted every day of the year. — $850.00

AMERICAN ELK (PURE)
From North America. Can be hunted Sept. 1 to Mar. 15 — $4,500.00

EUROPEAN RED STAG (PURE)
The most striking of European big game. Can be hunted Sept. 1 to Mar. 15 — $3,500.00

CORSICAN RAM
From Corsica. Can be hunted every day of year. — $500.00

CATALINA BUCKS
Can be hunted every day of the year. — $400.00

WILD TURKEY
Texas native. Can be hunted the Sat. nearest to the 15th of Nov. through Dec. 31 — $200.00

OTHER GAME:
Semitar Oryx – 2500
Gemsbok – 3000
American Buffalo – 2500
Barasigha Deer – 3000
Nilgai – 2000
Red Lechwe – 3500

**NO KILL
NO PAY GUARANTEE**

Hunting ranches provide an easy way for wealthy clients to bag animal heads to stuff and mount on their walls. Unfortunately, some retired zoo animals wind up on these ranches through carelessness on the part of those who attempt to find homes for them.

Occasionally animals from even reputable zoos have wound up on these ranches. This has been a source of enormous friction between animal rights groups and zoos. (For more on this subject see Chapter 8).

Few people are rich enough to afford the fees at one of these ranches and fewer still would regard this sort of activity as pleasurable. But the fact that there are enough rich and otherwise respectable men (few women hunt) who are willing to pay a lot of money for the sheer joy of killing something exotic, rare, or unusual is unsettling to say the least.

TRAPS AND "RANCHES"

5

At one time an outrageously expensive fur coat was the height of fashion, a symbol of wealth and success. One of the major fur companies had an advertising campaign featuring famous women wearing fur coats. The headline for the ad read "What Becomes a Legend." Even less affluent folk wore cheaper fur coats, to try to imitate the rich and famous people they admired.

Today, however, celebrities no longer flaunt their furs. Only the most callous can put on one of these once fashionable coats without a feeling of uneasiness and guilt.

The campaign against wearing fur began long before the animal rights movement existed. A variety of animal welfare and humane organizations had decried the wearing of fur, and conservation groups had been very successful in their fight against using furs from endangered species like tigers and leopards. But it was the animal rights activists with their energy and often abrasive confrontational tactics that really gave fur coats a well-deserved bad name.

In many ways fur was a perfect target. In today's world fur is no longer necessary for warmth. It has been replaced by a wide variety of warmer and far cheaper products. For those who still want a furry look there are perfectly acceptable fake furs.

Methods of obtaining furs are particularly horrible and obvious. When videotapes of the slaughter of baby seals were shown on television the world recoiled in shock. The seals were beaten to death. Bullet holes would have spoiled the fur. The fuzzy white baby seal, with its huge eyes and appealing expression, became a symbol for all the wanton cruelty to animals. Some nations were moved to ban or limit this kind of hunting. But most significantly the demand for sealskin products practically dried up. When confronted with the bloody reality of what it took to produce those luxurious coats, people didn't want them anymore.

A lot of furs come from animals trapped with steel leg-hold traps. Trappers insist that the steel trap is not as cruel a device as it appears to be. But when invited to put their own naked foot into a steel trap and then remain in it for a couple of days, which is what happens to trapped animals, they invariably decline the invitation. The steel leg-hold trap is every bit as painful as it looks. In addition to the "target" animals like foxes and raccoons, a large number of dogs and cats and what the trappers refer to as "trash" animals (animals that do not have marketable coats) fall victim to the traps. They are either released, badly maimed, or more commonly killed and discarded by the trapper.

The United States and Canada are among the few western nations that have not outlawed the merciless steel-jaw leg trap, pictured here.

The leg-hold trap has been banned in more than seventy countries. But only a few states in the United States have been enlightened enough to pass similar bans. Trapping is not economically very important, and there are not many trappers. But they are well organized and have managed to block attempts to ban the leg-hold trap in most states. Trappers have a whole variety of arguments to support their position. The most persistent is that trapping is "traditional." It is also inhumane and utterly unnecessary in the modern world.

About half the fur used commercially comes from animals that are raised on what are called "ranches" or "farms." If you get a mental picture of a bunch of mink roaming around a large fenced area you've got it wrong. The mink, foxes, and other essentially wild animals spend their entire short lives in small wire cages. Their feet never touch the ground. As soon as they mature they are killed. They live more like laboratory animals than farm animals. If anything, the fur "ranch" is crueler than the leghold trap. By the way, a lot of animals die for fur fashions. It takes the skins of over sixty mink to make even a small mink coat.

Animal rights activists attacked the fur industry in a variety of ways. Posters, leaflets, and other literature exposed the pain behind trapping and fur ranching. Fur salons were picketed, and fur coat wearers were insulted and occasionally even assaulted. Celebrities including Princess Diana of England announced publicly that they would refuse to wear furs anymore. These were the sort of fashion leaders who were once featured in fur ads. Sophisticated and effective antifur ads were produced. Major magazines would no longer run ads for fur products, and many stores including the giant Sears chain won't sell furs anymore. A milestone of sorts was reached in March 1990 when Harrods of London, England, perhaps the most famous department store in the world, closed its fur salon. "It's just not the done thing to wear a fur coat in public anymore," the store's spokesperson explained. "Harrods has to move with the times."

Fur prices have plunged, but even that couldn't bring back the customers, and major fur companies

Animals rights protesters go to great lengths to draw attention to their anger with the fur business. Here, demonstrators are dressed as dogs surrounding a large figure of Cruela, the character in the movie 101 Dalmations who threatens to make fur coats of all the dogs.

began going out of business. Fur industry journals report that the "harvest" of wild furs has dropped as much as eighty percent.

It's risky to predict trends, particularly in fashion. The fur business has had downturns before and has come back. But this one looks permanent, for there seems to have been a deep change in public attitudes toward wearing furs.

The fight against wearing leather products is less easy and does not represent such a clear moral choice. Certain skin products, such as snakeskin and alligator hide, come from animals that were specifically killed for their skins. But the majority of leather products come from cows, pigs, and other animals that were killed primarily for food. If you eat a hamburger should you still feel guilty about wearing a leather jacket?

For the animal rights advocate, who is also a vegetarian, the conflict does not arise. But there are many, many people concerned about animals who are not vegetarians, yet they still feel uncomfortable about wearing animal skins of any kind. Particularly since there are plenty of artificial replacements for leather.

Silk comes from the cocoon of the silkworm, which is actually the larvae of a moth. In order to get the fibers for silk the silkworm is killed. Do animal rights extend to insects? Many activists feel that they do, and they will not wear silk.

Even wool is not entirely a guilt-free product. Animal rights activists point out that sheep specially bred for their wool have unnaturally thick coats and may die of heat exhaustion in the summer or from exposure after they have been sheared. Shearing itself is a very uncomfortable experience for the sheep. The sheep also have their tails docked and their ears notched. They are, in short, regarded solely as "resources" rather than living and conscious creatures who are capable of feeling pain.

The most committed of the animal rights advocates stick strictly to cotton or artificial fibers.

PETS AND COMPANIONS

6

Most of us have shared our lives with a dog, cat, or some other animal. As a nation Americans spend more on pet food than baby food. Every year millions more are spent on veterinary care, leashes, catnip, flea powder, and other animal accessories. Americans love their pets. (Many animal rights supporters don't like the word pet, for it implies an animal is simply a piece of property. They prefer the term companion animal or companimal.)

But there is a sinister side to this love affair. More than half the over twenty million dogs and cats that are born in this country every year wind up in shelters and the vast majority of these animals are put to death within a few weeks or even days. The number of animals killed in shelters has been declining since the 1970s, but it is still enormous. Other unwanted animals are simply abandoned and live out short miserable lives in a world to which they are not adapted. This yearly destruction of millions of animals who have been bred to trust us and depend on us is the greatest single scandal in our treatment of animals. And it is a preventable tragedy.

The problem starts when people get animals for the wrong reasons or without thinking ahead. A puppy or kitten sounds like a nice gift for Christmas or a birthday. Perhaps there is an irresistibly cute puppy in a pet store window. Or a neighbor whose cat has just had kittens offers you "the pick of the litter."

But puppies grow into dogs that must be walked and fed regularly, and will probably chew up your favorite sneakers. Kittens become cats that will sharpen their claws on the furniture and throw up hairballs on the living room rug. Dogs and cats must have regular checkups and get shots. And when they get sick it can cost money—lots of money. A well-cared-for dog can live ten to fifteen years; cats can live even longer.

When a dog or cat becomes too difficult or inconvenient, too many people fool themselves into thinking that the animal can be taken to a "shelter" from which it will be adopted by a loving family. The truth is that the animal, particularly an adult animal, will almost certainly spend a few days in a cage and then be killed. There are far, far more animals that need homes than there are homes that want animals. It is an even worse and crueler deception to think the animal can be turned out onto the streets or in the country and be able to take care of itself. Abandoning an animal that way condemns it to a short life and an awful death.

The problem is made worse when people fail to have their animals "fixed"; that is, spayed or neutered, so that they can't have more puppies or kit-

There are hundreds of thousands of adorable cats and dogs in animal shelters across the United States, all awaiting adoption. Taking in an animal is a major commitment and there are nowhere near enough families willing or able to care for the animal population.

tens. Spaying and neutering is troublesome: You have to make an appointment with the vet, it costs money, there is some pain for the animal, and since it's an operation there is always a small risk. Some people also think that it's a good idea for a female animal to have at least one litter. Parents may believe this will help explain "the miracle of birth" to their children. They are always sure that they can find good homes for the puppies or kittens. Failing that they can be taken to the shelter, where they will surely be adopted. Given the enormous annual slaughter of unwanted dogs and cats not one of these reasons or excuses holds up for a moment. If you have a dog or cat that hasn't been fixed then you risk contributing to the terrible overpopulation problem.

You have probably heard all of this before, though it is worth repeating. Everyone who cares about animals agrees on these basic points. Now let's move on to some more controversial questions.

Where do you get a companion animal? The pet store is a nearly legendary American institution. There is that old song about the "doggie in the window" and those pictures of freckle-faced kids looking at happy puppies. It's hard to walk into a pet shop without walking out with one of those lovable bundles of fur and fun.

But ask yourself, where do all these puppies come from? The answer is not pleasant. Most pet shop puppies come from places that have been dubbed "puppy mills." These are large kennels, located primarily in midwestern states, where dogs are bred like cattle. Conditions for puppy mill dogs are simply awful. When they are just a few weeks old the puppies are crated up and shipped off all over the country. Many do not survive the trip. Puppy mills exist only in places where humane treatment laws are weak and where there is little inspection or enforcement. They are a disgrace, and they could and should be shut down.

Pet shop puppies are often ill and can have serious genetic defects. Because they have been so badly treated during critical periods of their lives they can grow up to be timid, nervous, or vicious. Almost all puppies are friendly; their real behavior becomes apparent only after they mature. A cute puppy that turns out to be a snappy, noisy, and untrainable dog is the sort that winds up in an animal shelter. Pet shop puppies are usually sold "with papers." That means the puppies are registered with the American Kennel Club (AKC), and that's all they mean. The papers are no guarantee of health or temperament. They are not even a guarantee that the dog is a good representative of its breed, and since there is a great deal of fraud in registering puppies, they are no guarantee that the puppy is even a representative of a particular breed at all.

Pet shops encourage impulse buying—the worst way to get a pet. What can you do? Don't buy animals in a pet shop. Don't buy pet supplies in any shop that sells dogs, cats, exotic birds, reptiles, or any wild-caught animals. It's a bad idea to try to keep any wild animal as a pet and those that are sold in pet shops, particularly the birds, are caught, shipped, and kept under terrible conditions. If pet shops that sell animals don't make money they will either stop selling animals or shut down completely. That would spell an end for puppy mills and the cruel wild animal trade.

If you want a companion dog where should you go? Animal rights groups will tell you to go to a shelter and adopt a dog that might otherwise be killed. There is a great deal to be said for this suggestion. But what if you want a particular breed of dog?

Many animal rights groups are not comfortable with the idea of purebred dogs. Indeed a few don't like the idea of any sort of companion animal. They believe all animals should be free, not subservient to humans. They certainly don't like the idea of dogs being bred to suit human fashions and fancies. And they say that purebred dogs have a lot of inherited defects and diseases.

It is true that certain kinds of purebred dogs do have genetic problems. Short-nosed breeds have breathing difficulties, and many of the larger breeds are prone to a potentially crippling malformation of the hindquarters called hip dysplasia. However, the most severe problems usually occur in pet shop or puppy mill dogs. And mixed breeds are by no means free of inherited problems.

The best reason for getting a purebred dog is that you have a much better chance of knowing what that cute little puppy is going to look like and act like when it grows up. Getting a good purebred dog is not something that should be done on impulse. It takes work and patience.

First, you have to locate someone who breeds the particular kind of dog you are interested in. The American Kennel Club will supply you with a list of breeders in your area. A reputable breeder will not try to sell you a dog. You have to convince the breeder that you are worthy of having one of his or her dogs. You should make at least one visit to the kennel so that you can see the conditions under which the dogs are kept. If the place is overcrowded or dirty, forget it. You should be able to meet a pup's mother and father. That's the best way of determining what a puppy will look and act like when it grows up. You will probably have to wait until a suitable puppy is available, and of course many purebred dogs are expensive. But if you get the right dog it's more than worth the trouble. A good breeder will usually agree to take back a dog at any time. You may not get your money returned unless there is something seriously wrong with the dog, but at least it won't wind up waiting for death in a shelter.

The bulldog is an example of what many animal rights activists feel is wrong with purebred dogs. Once bred for the brutal sport of bullbaiting, the modern bulldog is a caricature of its fighting ancestor. All the viciousness has been bred out of them, and certain characteristics like the large head and pushed-in face have been exaggerated. The bulldog's head is so large that puppies almost always have to be born by cesarean. The adult bulldog has breathing problems and often suffers from bad hips and back legs. The bulldog is about as "unnatural" an animal as one can imagine; it couldn't survive without constant human care and attention. Yet there are thousands of people in America who dote on these lovable, misshapen creatures, and who will spend enormous sums of money to keep them as healthy and happy as possible.

Bulldogs rarely wind up abandoned in shelters. And if they do chances are very good that they will be adopted, or "rescued," by people devoted to the breed. A lot of breed clubs have "rescue committees" that do this sort of work. It is therefore reasonable to ask if the "unnatural" bulldog is worse off than some healthy mutt who is destined to become one of the millions of unwanted dogs that are destroyed every year.

Animal rights supporters and purebred dog enthusiasts are in open conflict in several areas. There is the practice of "docking" the tails and "cropping" the ears of dogs. In many breeds, the Doberman pinscher, for example, the tails are cut off and the ears surgically altered to make them assume an unnatural position. While at one time there may have been a practical reason for shortening a dog's tail, today it's for appearance. Tail docking is done when a puppy is just a few days old and breeders insist that it doesn't hurt the puppy, or doesn't hurt very much. There don't seem to be any long-term negative effects on dogs from either of these procedures, but there are no positive effects either as far as the dog is concerned. The operations have been banned in many European countries and the betting is that cropping and docking will be banned in the United States within the next ten years. A lot of popular breeds are going to look different, but the dogs will probably be better off.

The more radical animal rights supporters actively oppose dog shows, which they regard as both cruel and degrading to the dogs. Dog shows can be exhausting and confining, but to say that they are cruel is stretching the definition. There are documented examples of cruelty at dog shows, but these are rare. The vast majority of those who show dogs genuinely love them. Unlike racehorses and racing greyhounds, which are put to death when their "ca-

Many dog lovers breed and train their purebred animals for dog shows. Certain groups within the animal rights movement feel that such shows exploit the dogs. The debate rages on with no solution.

reers" are over, the show dog usually retires to life as a family pet. A poodle in full show clip does look silly, but it is doubtful that the dog feels degraded. There are rumors that animal rights activists have from time to time "liberated" dogs from their crates at shows. But it is difficult to determine how often this happens. No animal rights organization openly advocates such actions.

The enormous number of dogs and cats that are destroyed each year has led to a legal response. In 1990 the Humane Society of San Mateo County, California, proposed an ordinance that would ban the breeding of all dogs and cats in the county. The humane society said that each year its shelter euthanizes, or kills, seven thousand cats and three thousand dogs. They hoped a breeding ban would help to cut down the numbers of unwanted animals. The society also invited local TV news cameras in to televise a dog being euthanized. This dramatic gesture was to bring the grim reality of the situation home to the public in the most graphic way possible.

The gesture certainly captured public attention. The proposed San Mateo ordinance got nationwide publicity and sparked interest in lots of other communities faced with the same terrible problem. Animal rights groups, which generally support measures that humanely limit animal populations, backed the San Mateo ordinance. The AKC and most purebred-dog breeders were horrified. They said that the regulations would only hurt responsible dog breeders. Puppy mills already operate in areas that traditionally resist any kind of legislation regulating animal breeding. Irresponsible people who let their dogs and cats breed freely are not going to be influenced by any local ordinance. Dog owners and breeders quickly organized throughout the country to fight such restrictions, and so far they have been successful. Even the San Mateo ordinance, when it was finally passed, did not call for a breeding ban.

The dog people are probably right, and San Mateo-type ordinances will do little or nothing to reduce the population of unwanted animals. But the publicity it generated did force the public to pay greater attention to the problem of pet overpopulation. It also forced some changes in the AKC. This powerful organization was once concerned strictly with show dogs. Recently, however, the organization has expressed a lot more interest in dogs in general. And that is a good thing.

The animal rights movement has raised a number of difficult and uncomfortable questions regarding those animals that we call our pets. As in so many other areas, there are few easy answers.

THAT'S ENTERTAINMENT?

7

From racehorses to Lassie, animals have been an important part of human entertainment. Today there is both good news and bad news for animals used in sports and entertainment.

The good news is that some of the worst and cruelest abuses have been reduced because of public pressure. For example, movies that once routinely allowed horses to be maimed and killed in filming Westerns are now rigidly regulated, at least in the United States. The bad news is that the abuses of animals in entertainment have not been completely eliminated and in at least one area abusive practices have become more common.

The rodeo, which was popular mainly in the American Southwest, seemed to be dying out ten or fifteen years ago. But then cable television, eager to fill its time with new and inexpensive "sports," began showing rodeos. Television gave the rodeo new life, and now rodeos travel all over the country, attracting large and profitable crowds. Rodeos gross millions every year.

Rodeos are often billed as "healthy family entertainment," and promoters are very sensitive to charges that rodeo animals are abused. The promoters insist that the horses, bulls, and other animals are well fed and cared for. "Why would we want to harm a valuable animal?" they say.

In fact, there are very few regulations governing the treatment of rodeo animals. Small or marginal rodeos neglect even basic standards of care. In the end it is cheaper to get a new animal than properly care for an older or injured one. But even if the animals were properly cared for this defense misses the point. The rodeo is a show based on cruelty.

Why do you think the "bucking bronco" or "wild bull" act the way they do? Is it because they are so fierce and untamed? Not at all. They are forced to wear a thick leather strap across the flanks that is painfully tightened, causing them to buck and rear. If you were strapped up that way you'd jump too. As soon as the strap is loosened the animals calm down. Just for a little extra "kick" they are often given a shock with an electric cattle prod to make them bolt out of the chute.

In calf roping a terrified young animal, running over 20 miles (32 kilometers) an hour, is brought to a sudden halt by a rope that has been tossed around its neck. It is then slammed to the ground and tied up. Injuries are common, and the inevitable fate of all of these animals is the slaughterhouse.

Eliminate the flank straps, the cattle prods, the calf roping, and all the other abusive practices, and there would be no rodeo. The image the rodeo tries to create is one of "brave" men taming "savage" beasts. The savagery, however, is all on the side of the men. There is nothing uplifting about watching animals in fear and pain.

Some rodeo defenders say that it is a "traditional" activity, and since it is part of our historical heritage it should be preserved. There are a lot of "traditional" practices, from dueling to child labor, that have not been preserved, and for good reasons. The only reason that rodeos survive to this day is because some people can make money on them.

What can you do? First, and obviously, if a rodeo comes to your town don't go, and urge all your friends and relatives not to go. Often rodeos are sponsored by local charities, business groups, and even schools. Contact the sponsors and remind them of the cruelty that is at the heart of the rodeo. Most people don't know or don't think about it. Write to your local newspaper objecting to the rodeo. Write to TV networks that show rodeos. Write to companies whose products are advertised during the rodeo shows. One letter is not going to stop a rodeo. But if sponsors keep hearing from people, it's going to make them wonder if they shouldn't put their advertising dollars elsewhere.

Another old American entertainment institution that regularly abuses animals is the circus. The circus is no longer what it once was. There is only one large circus, Ringling Brothers and Barnum and Bailey, and a number of small ones, which generally tour rural areas and small towns.

While cruelty is not central to the circus, there is no doubt that circus animals live miserable lives. They are trucked from place to place in tiny cages,

> When an animal is performing, perhaps in
> a spangly costume, it may appear to have a
> glamorous life—but behind the scenes the life
> of a circus animal is very sad.

and in the smaller circuses are often poorly fed and
not given adequate veterinary care. Training is often
brutal. And once again the message of the circus
animal act is human domination over the "savage
beast." Many of these "beasts," by the way, have had
their claws or teeth surgically removed, just in case
they really do turn on their tormentors. And when
an animal becomes too old or injured to perform it is
rarely allowed to go into a comfortable retirement. It
may be sent on to an even worse circus, or to a game
farm, where it is shot for "sport."

There is a genuine romance to the circus, and there are now a number of circuses like The Cirque du Soleil that don't use animal acts. If you want to go to the circus that's the kind to go to. If one of the old-fashioned circuses shows up in your town, partic-ularly if it is sponsored by a local civic organization or charity, speak up. If people don't go to the circus, it won't come to town anymore, and that would be just fine.

County fairs sometimes feature a "diving" horse or mule. The animal is walked up onto a high plat-form and pushed into a tank of water. That is sup-posed to be entertaining! Schools often sponsor an event called "donkey basketball" as a fund-raiser. The animals are kicked around, prodded, and beaten, and then trucked off to the next town for the next performance. If people really thought about what they were watching, they probably wouldn't go. As with the rodeo and the circus, speak up and make people think. Unlike a lot of animal cruelty these activities are marginal. If enough people care it would not be hard to put them out of business for-ever.

The most obvious form of animal cruelty, dog-fights, have long been illegal. Dogfights still take place in some parts of the country, particularly the rural South and some inner city areas. If you happen to hear about dogfights being staged in your area notify the police or the local humane society. The people who do this are criminals and their activities can be dangerous to humans as well as other ani-mals.

Cockfighting, which is pitting two roosters fit-ted with steel spurs against one another in a fight to the death, is popular in many parts of the world. Immigrants from South and Central America, the Philippines, and other places bring the practice with them and stage illegal cockfights. But there are at least six states where cockfighting is not illegal, although it generally operates secretively, and a lot of illegal gambling does take place. Humane societies and animal rights groups are working hard to make this barbaric practice a felony everywhere.

Some areas sponsor events like rattlesnake hunts, pigeon shoots, and even rabbit-killing spectacles. They are justified as being "traditional" or even as "family fun." "If the kids are out here killing rabbits," sponsors insist, "they won't be out taking drugs." Is there no other choice? These justifications don't hold up, not for a moment. When a large number of people become aware of what is going on, these cruel practices tend to fade away or are outlawed. Animal rights groups now stage noisy and effective protests at such events.

Horse racing is not an inherently cruel sport; that is, killing or abusing an animal is not central to the event. Winning racehorses are extremely valuable animals and are generally well treated. But not all racehorses are winners, and those that do not race well, or become too old, or are injured are generally killed. Racehorses are specially bred for speed not durability. Their legs are very light for such a large animal, and they often break under the pounding they receive during a race. Despite all the romance that has traditionally been attached to horse racing there is still a cruel side to the sport.

The racehorse, however, has a wonderful life when compared with the usual fate of the racing greyhound. Dogs are far easier to breed and keep than horses, so there are plenty of greyhounds available. The racing greyhound generally has a "career" that lasts two or three years, most of the time spent in small kennels or crates. After that it is either killed or sold to a laboratory for research. Recently there has been a hopeful development. Under the urging of a small number of greyhound lovers, some trainers and owners have allowed their older racing dogs to be adopted as pets. These large, kennel-bred dogs make surprisingly gentle and affectionate companions. However, because they are so large and need a place to run, a "retired" greyhound is not for everyone. Despite its success, the greyhound adoption program cannot save all, or even the majority, of the animals from an early death.

Performing dolphins, or other marine mammals, have become increasingly popular attractions. The shows that allow people, for a fee, to swim in the tank with captive dolphins are not a good idea and should be avoided completely. Attractions where dolphins are kept isolated in small tanks should also be avoided. There is nothing entertaining about seeing an animal in solitary confinement.

The large and extremely popular marine parks, like Seaworld, are not so easy to condemn. Like prize racehorses, the trained dolphins and killer whales in these attractions are physically well treated. There is also no doubt that these attractions have helped to raise public consciousness about dolphins and other marine mammals and have made people more willing to support laws that protect wild dolphins. Unlike the rodeo, which serves to reinforce the domination of the human animal over other animals,

Like dog shows, dolphin shows are the center of a debate. Are the performing animals happy in their roles as well cared for stars—or would they prefer their natural open-water environment?

dolphin shows tend to make us appreciate the intelligence of these remarkable creatures, even if they are trained to perform some rather silly stunts. The marine parks have also contributed a lot to our knowledge of dolphins.

Animal rights activists insist that confining these large free-ranging animals, even under the best of conditions, places them under unbearable stress. The marine parks say there is no evidence of this and that their animals are happy and healthy. It's impossible to see a good dolphin show without a sense of wonder and amazement. But it's difficult not to feel uneasy as well. Are these friendly animals that appear to be smiling all the time really as happy as they look?

TIMMY AND HIS FRIEND

8

In the autumn of 1991, Timmy, a thirty-two-year-old male lowland gorilla, was scheduled to be sent from the Cleveland Metro Park Zoo, where he had spent most of his life, to the Bronx Zoo in New York City. The transfer was to be made for breeding purposes. For eighteen months Timmy had shared an enclosure with Katie, a young female gorilla. While the two got along quite well, the female had never become pregnant, and veterinarians found her reproductive system did not function properly. At the Bronx Zoo Timmy would be housed with four fertile female gorillas. In the wild, male gorillas have harems. The hope was that these females would produce Timmy's offspring.

The lowland gorilla is one of many endangered species. A primary task of today's major zoos is breeding endangered species. For some species the zoo is the last best hope for survival. A great drawback in a captive-breeding program is that a small number of animals will be bred over and over again.

At the request of the gorilla Species Survival
Plan, Timmy, a male lowland gorilla was
sent to the Bronx Zoo from the Cleveland
Metroparks Zoo in order to be introduced to
a number of potential mates.

A lot of offspring can be produced, but they will
share a very limited gene pool, which can be potentially disastrous for long-term survival.

Timmy had been caught in the wild some thirty
years earlier. Today there is a ban on the capture of
wild gorillas. All the new gorillas in zoos are born
there. Timmy was not directly related to any other
zoo gorilla. For that reason zoo officials considered it
very important for Timmy to be bred.

The people of Cleveland were saddened when they heard that this very popular resident of their zoo was going to be shipped off to New York. Some animal rights groups were more than saddened; they were absolutely outraged. They said it was cruel to take Timmy away from his familiar surroundings and his companion Katie. They said that the stress of this change could harm his health. And they went to court to try to stop the transfer. The incident got an enormous amount of publicity. In court the animal rights groups lost their case. The judge decided that it was in the gorilla's best interest to go to the Bronx. He arrived in New York in November 1991 and at last report was adjusting very well to his new surroundings.

It might seem that zoo professionals, who are devoted to the preservation of endangered species, and supporters of animal rights would be natural allies. The case of Timmy the gorilla is a small but revealing example of the sort of conflicts that have developed between the two groups. But first let's look at the important areas in which both sides agree.

Today there are approximately 1,500 places in the country that are identified as zoos. Of these, only one tenth—about 150—are members of the American Association of Zoological Parks and Aquariums (AAZPA). The AAZPA sets standards for the display and treatment of animals in all member institutions. If an institution doesn't meet the standards it doesn't get into the AAZPA. Most of the major zoos like the Bronx Zoo and the Cleveland Zoo are AAZPA members. Of those that are not members the vast majority can be classified as "roadside zoos."

Typically a roadside zoo is a small place with a name like TRADER BOB'S RATTLESNAKE PIT or HAPPYLAND PETTING ZOO. There are more roadside zoos in states like Florida that are warm and have lots of tourists, but they can be found anywhere. Most roadside zoos display a small number of animals in wire cages or some sort of concrete enclosures. Domestic and semidomestic animals like llamas are most common, as are native American species like bears and raccoons. Sometimes a more exotic animal like a lion or monkey may be in the collection, but such zoos rarely have genuinely endangered species. Animals may be available to be petted, fed, or ridden by young visitors. These places may seem like fun to visit, but they are nothing more than prisons for animals. Furthermore, sometimes animals can be literally petted to death.

The roadside zoo is strictly a money-making venture. Some of the owners of these zoos may really love the animals they display, but they never have enough space and are often forced to cut corners on adequate veterinary care and even food.

The message that the roadside zoo sends is all wrong. Here animals are treated simply as objects for human entertainment. What's entertaining about a bear, driven mad by confinement, pacing back and forth in a tiny cage? The roadside zoo is an institution that should no longer exist. It's a relic of an earlier era.

What can you do about them? Simple, don't go. Once people stop paying admission the roadside zoos will wither away. If your friends or family are taking a vacation tell them not to patronize these places. If your school is planning a field trip to the zoo, find out if that particular zoo is a member of the AAZPA. If it's not, see if you can get your teacher to reschedule the trip to a member zoo or to a museum or park.

But Timmy wasn't being sent to a rundown roadside zoo. He was being sent to the Bronx Zoo, generally regarded as the best zoo in the United States and perhaps the best zoo in the world. Nor was he being sent simply to amuse Bronx Zoo visitors. He was part of a very carefully structured plan to save endangered species. Why then did some animal rights activists object to the transfer of Timmy?

At the extreme there are those who oppose all zoos. They think it is morally wrong to keep any animal in captivity, no matter what the circumstances. Ingrid Newkirk, founder and director of People for the Ethical Treatment of Animals (PETA), wants to see all zoos closed down so animals "will get to stay in their homes."

Zoos are accused of a variety of sins. The most persistent is that animals confined in zoos suffer horribly because they are not allowed to lead "natural" lives. There is some truth to this charge. Even the very best of today's zoos still have some bad exhibits. Visitors to highly rated zoos can still see elephants that are kept chained part of the time or a naturally sociable animal like a chimpanzee isolated in a cage or enclosure.

Zoos are well aware of these problems. Elephants are among the most difficult animals to keep. They are extremely large, very strong, and can be unpredictable and dangerous. Every year zookeepers are killed or severely injured by elephants. It's a risk they are willing to take. In nature elephants live in large herds that travel over hundreds of square miles. There is no way to approximate that in a zoo. But zoos are trying. The Washington Park Zoo in Portland, Oregon, specializes in elephants and has been reasonably successful at keeping and breeding elephants in a series of large enclosures.

Would the elephants be better off in "the wild"? Almost certainly. But for elephants there is not enough "wild" left. In Africa and Asia the elephant herds are being squeezed into ever smaller areas by an expanding human population. The herds are decimated by poachers. Elephants are now an endangered species. The realistic choice for the elephants is not if they would be better off in the wild, but if they would be better off dead.

How about that lonely chimpanzee? Zoo professionals realize that chimps are sociable animals and try to allow them to live in family groups as much as possible, just as they do in nature. But sometimes a chimpanzee, usually an older male, will become so aggressive that he becomes a positive danger to others. In the wild the other chimps would have the space to successfully avoid him. In zoo confinement he has to be isolated. Once again the question is whether he would be better off dead.

Serious questions have been raised about keeping large marine mammals in captivity, particularly the killer whale, or orca. These very large animals have become extremely popular performers at a number of commercial marine attractions. Although the captive killer whales are treated well physically there is some evidence to suggest that the stresses of captivity are very hard for them. Moreover, they are not at present an endangered species, and they do not breed well in captivity anyway. There may be

In the past, zoos meant animals in cages. Modern zoos try to exhibit animals under conditions that match as closely as possible the way the animals lived in the wild.

species that should not be kept in captivity, and the killer whale may be one of them.

Another charge leveled against zoos is that they sell "surplus" animals to commercial hunting ranches, where they are shot, to roadside zoos, laboratories, circuses, or other places where they are exploited. The AAZPA has a firm policy against the sale of zoo animals to unacceptable places like hunting ranches, but in fact, such sales do take place. Some zoos, including some of the country's most respected, have sold animals to animal dealers, who in turn sell them to the highest bidder, which may happen to be a hunting ranch. In January 1990 the popular TV show *60 Minutes* had a segment on how some animals from the famous San Diego Zoo wound up on hunting ranches. The report turned out to be accurate, and not only San Diego but the entire zoo community was badly hurt. More than anything else zoos depend on public support.

How widespread are such practices? It's hard to say, but they are not nearly as common as antizoo activists would like the public to believe. No zoo deliberately raises animals for sale, but space in a zoo is always at a premium. What does a zoo do when it has more animals of a particular species than it has room for? The best thing to do is send the extra animals to a good zoo that does have room. That is not always possible. Some zoos humanely kill these "surplus" animals. It's a tough decision, and one which outrages animal rights activists and upsets ordinary zoogoers. But if the only other choice is to send them to a hunting ranch or a similar horror then it is also the right decision.

Other charges leveled against zoos are simply untrue. PETA says that large numbers of wild animals are captured for zoos and "up to 10 adult animals may be killed to capture one young animal for a zoo." That may have been true fifty years ago. Today eighty percent of the mammals in zoos were born in captivity, and fifty percent are third- or fourth-generation captive born. These captive-born animals are not really "wild" animals at all. Zoos have strict regulations against importing any endangered species. Are these rules sometimes violated? Almost certainly, but it is not a common practice, and far more mammals are born in zoos than brought to them.

Another charge is that zoo animals are exploited, made to perform undignified tricks or forced to undergo the stresses of endless petting from children. Animal performances of one kind or another were once fairly common in major zoos, but not anymore. Occasionally some animals like elephants and sea lions are trained to do routines, but zookeepers insist that the routines help the animals to overcome boredom and give veterinarians a chance to look closely at the animals. Visitor entertainment is secondary.

The animals in the children's zoo area of most major zoos are carefully protected. Generally if they are annoyed they can walk away, though they rarely seem to. They also "work" very short hours. It's important to remember that many of the people who oversee this part of the zoo are docents or volunteers—they are there strictly because they love animals just as much as the animal rights activists do. In fact, even the professionals who work in zoos do it for the love of animals. Being a zookeeper is a hard job with long hours and low pay. These are not the sort of people who would stand for animal abuse.

Another charge is that zoos take taxpayers' money that could better be spent on protecting wild populations. Most major zoos run at a loss that is made up by private donations and tax funds. Even if zoos disappeared there is no reason to believe that the money would go into wildlife conservation. Most major zoos also sponsor conservation projects throughout the world and contribute far more money to wildlife conservation than do all the anti-zoo activists.

One of the most well publicized zoo projects, returning captive-bred animals to their natural habitats, has been attacked as an expensive failure. Returning captive-bred animals to the wild is expensive, and very few species have been helped this way. Zoo professionals acknowledge that the key to preserving endangered species is protecting their habitats, not returning them to a wild that may no longer exist. But some species have been saved this way. Were it not for the Bronx Zoo, the American bison, commonly known as the buffalo, would have become extinct in the early years of the twentieth century. More recently, animals from the California condor to the little monkey called the golden lion tamarin have been returned to the wild from captivity. Captive breeding cannot save the majority of endangered species, but it can save a few. If zoos had strong captive-breeding programs a century ago the passenger pigeon would never have become extinct.

A large part of the controversy boils down to basic differences in outlook. Animal rights supporters are interested in the individual animal. That's why they worried about moving Timmy. Zoo professionals worry more about the entire species. Would Timmy's move contribute to the overall population of a threatened species? He might be happier as well, but it was the species they were most concerned about.

Animal rights supporters also have an attitude about "nature" that zoo professionals and others find romantic and unrealistic. Animals in the wild do not live pleasant and pain-free lives. They face hunger, disease, parasites, and in the end the probability of being killed and eaten by another animal. Anyone who has watched films of a lion bringing down a zebra, or of an aging lion being attacked by a pack of hyenas, knows that most often death in nature is terrifying. Zoo animals usually live longer and healthier lives than their wild counterparts, and they have more offspring.

Even more basically, many animal rights advocates fail to recognize that what we call "nature" or "the wild" doesn't really exist anymore, certainly not for large mammals. Increasingly, large mammals live only in carefully protected parks and reserves. And these areas are under constant pressure from an ever-growing human population. The rat and the cockroach have fully adapted to a human-dominated world and do quite well on their own. The grizzly bear and black rhino will survive only as long as human beings are willing to make sacrifices to allow them to survive.

One of the great missions of the modern zoo is to educate its visitors about conservation. No one can visit a major zoo anywhere in the United States without having the message of conservation driven home time after time. Even more important is the fact that a zoo offers most people their only chance to see most animal species alive. Watching a nature video is not the same as seeing a living animal. Few zoo patrons will have the opportunity to visit the national parks of Africa or even Alaska. Perhaps the settings are not "natural" but the animals are real enough. By getting close to real animals people come to love them. And they will support efforts to save the rain forests or protect wilderness areas from further commercial exploitation.

Those in the animal rights movement who campaign against zoos wind up hurting the very animals they are so determined to protect.

THE INDIVIDUAL OR THE SPECIES

9

Usually respect for animal rights and the preservation of wild species, particularly endangered species, are points of view that support one another. Animal rights advocates have been among the leaders in the fight to preserve endangered species and the habitats upon which they depend. In many ways the animal rights movement is a child of the ecology movement. But occasionally those who regard themselves as conservationists and animal rights advocates can come sharply and painfully in conflict with one another.

Let's look at the case of Round Island, a small island in the Indian Ocean. At one time it was completely covered with forest. But in the 1880s domestic rabbits and goats were released on the island to provide food for sailors who might become stranded there. The domestic species adapted so well to their new environment that they ate up nearly all the vegetation, right down to the roots. Without plants to hold it, a lot of the island's topsoil washed away. As a result several species of snakes and lizards that occur nowhere else in the world were threatened with extinction.

In the late 1970s the government of Mauritius, which controls the island, decided to try to save the endangered species by getting rid of the rabbits and goats. The first plan was to drop poison bait on the island. But this produced a huge international protest, for that would condemn all who ate it to a slow and painful death.

After some discussion a marksman was hired to shoot the goats. This is not a solution that would be acceptable to most animal rights advocates today. They would suggest trapping the goats and transporting them somewhere else, or perhaps sterilizing them somehow, so they could not reproduce and would die out naturally. These solutions are expensive, and they don't always work. Goats are notoriously hard to trap. And once you have trapped a semiwild goat what do you do with it? You certainly couldn't release it among the farms of nearby Mauritius, because the farmers would shoot it immediately. In any event the marksman shot all but one of the goats. But the rabbits remained.

A number of suggestions for getting rid of the rabbits were considered, including a fast-acting poison gas. But for one reason or another they were all rejected. Ultimately the rabbits were eradicated from the island by a combination of shooting, trapping, and poison. One of the endangered snakes had already become extinct, but the island's vegetation has been recovering, and there is hope for the other threatened species.

The more radical animal rights advocates would argue that what was done on Round Island was completely immoral. In this view a member of an endangered species, like the Round Island snake, has no more right to live and avoid suffering than a member of a species that is quite numerous, like the rabbit. No matter how good the intentions, they say, it is simply wrong to painfully kill one for the sake of the other. It is the rights of the individual animal that are paramount. Besides, people brought the rabbits and goats to the island in the first place. Now people were killing them off to correct that earlier mistake. What was done on Round Island and in other places has been labeled "environmental fascism."

Many others who consider themselves supporters of animal rights would probably agree that it is vital to save an endangered species from extinction even if other animals have to suffer. But they would almost certainly feel that not enough had been done to treat the goats and rabbits of Round Island in a humane manner.

Conservationists, whose primary aim is preserving species and ecosystems, not individual animals, say that there just weren't enough time or resources available to remove the goats and rabbits to some other place. As it was, the delay probably resulted in the extinction of a species of snake.

As you can see, the problems raised by a place like Round Island are not easy ones. They are certainly not limited to an obscure island in the Indian Ocean. But fortunately the stories don't always end with the killing of animals.

Burros were brought to North America by the Spanish in the sixteenth century. Some of them escaped and went wild. They prospered in the American Southwest. In fact, they have done so well that in some places they have pushed out native wildlife and have destroyed fragile desert ecosystems. Feral burros became so destructive in Grand Canyon National Park that park authorities announced plans to shoot them. When that plan was announced it created a major uproar among animal lovers.

Instead of just complaining, however, one national animal protection organization, The Fund for Animals, was able to raise the money to finance a campaign to have the burros captured and taken out of the park. Many of the burros were adopted. Both the ecosystem and the burros were saved.

This is not a solution that is going to work everywhere. Burros are extremely sturdy animals. They endure capture and confinement very well. Many other species are very hard to capture and move. A large percentage of them may be injured or killed. And usually no one knows what to do with the animals after they have been captured. Even the burro rescue program had its critics. It was expensive; it cost about $500,000 to move six hundred burros. Critics say the money and effort might be put to better use to preserve other types of animals. The critics also point out that campaigns to save animals that are "cute" like burros are far more popular with the public than campaigns to save snakes or toads or other animals that are not considered "cute."

Wild animal "overpopulation" presents another area of potential conflict between supporters of animal rights and conservationists. The goats and rabbits of Round Island and the burros of Grand Canyon National Park were not natives but were introduced by humans. Sometimes, however, there are too many native animals in a region. In reality this is not so much a problem of animal "overpopulation" as it is of human "overpopulation." As human beings take over ever-larger areas of the planet, wild animals are forced into smaller habitats, sometimes habitats that are not able to sustain them properly. Perhaps the most dramatic and tragic example of this is what has happened to the elephant.

Throughout most of their range in both Asia and Africa, elephants are a seriously endangered species. Large portions of their habitats have been destroyed. And even in those places where they are supposed to be protected, governments have been too poor and weak to properly shield these wonderful creatures from ivory poachers. By international agreement most nations have now banned the sale of ivory and other products made from elephants.

In some places, like national parks and reserves in South Africa and Zimbabwe, poaching has been effectively stopped and elephant herds have prospered. But the boundaries of the parks are limited, and when a large number of these huge and hungry creatures are squeezed into a relatively small area they will soon turn a forest into a desert. The solution proposed by most conservationists is culling—or to put it more bluntly—killing a certain number of elephants every year to keep down the size of the herd.

That is a "solution" to which animal rights activists and a lot of other people object very strongly. Since elephants are endangered, why can't they just be moved somewhere else? But it is not easy to capture and move an animal as large as an elephant. Remember we are talking here about wild African elephants, not the relatively docile, captive-bred elephants that are seen in most zoos. And where are they to be released? If they are taken to places where elephant populations have already been decimated by poachers, the only thing that has been accomplished is to provide more prey for the poacher. If poaching could be stopped, then the local elephant populations would recover.

Those nations that have large elephant herds want to sell ivory and other elephant products on the international market. They say they could use the money to help preserve the elephant's habitat. They also point out that if local people could look upon elephants as a potential source of income, rather than as a competitor for land, they would be far more interested in protecting the herds from poaching. When people are very poor, as they are in much of Africa and many other parts of the world, they do not have the luxury of worrying about saving endangered species. They have to worry about finding enough to eat. If the elephant herds provide them with money they will have a great incentive to preserve the elephants. On the other hand, there is no way of telling if a piece of ivory comes from an elephant legally culled from a large herd or from an elephant poached in an area where the animals have nearly disappeared. At the present time most nations believe that the ban on ivory and other elephant products should be continued.

This is not solely an elephant problem. The American alligator is one of the great success stories of conservation. Not too long ago the alligator faced extinction in Florida. But a ban on hunting and attempts to save at least some alligator habitat has brought this ancient and hardy creature back. Now alligators are turning up on golf courses and even in people's yards. There have been reports of alligators devouring the family pet. As a result, limited alligator hunting has been reintroduced.

In Australia the kangaroo does not face extinction. In fact it is so numerous that it competes very successfully with the herds of sheep that are so important to Australia's economy. A lot of Australian ranchers would like to "harvest" kangaroos; that is, kill a certain number of them and sell the meat and hides. But in America most people wouldn't touch kangaroo meat and would not be willing to buy products made from kangaroo leather.

To animal rights proponents, killing animals simply because they have become a nuisance to human beings is immoral. Some have said that rather than turning an intelligent and social animal like an elephant into a "renewable resource" to be "harvested" like so much corn, they would rather see the elephant become extinct.

That is a position that the philosophers of the animal rights movement have been able to argue logically and with great force. But does it make sense in the real world?

WHAT KIND OF WORLD?

10

Can you imagine a world in which no one ate meat or eggs, where no one wore furs, leather, or even wool? In the supermarket the consumer would have to check the ingredients of every product from breakfast cereal to shampoo to make sure that it contained nothing that came from an animal. No products, no drugs, no surgical techniques would be tested on animals, under any circumstances. There would certainly be no hunting, and quite probably no fishing. There would be no circuses, or at least no circus animals, and no zoos. There would be no pets, or companion animals. All of these animals would have been "phased out." Indeed there would be no domestic animals of any kind. If you wanted to enjoy the company of an animal it would have to be at a distance.

It's difficult to imagine such a world. Yet this is just the sort of world dreamed of by the more radical leaders of the animal rights movement. They envision this world as sort of a new Eden, a perfect world where the human species does not exploit any other animal species.

A lot of opponents of animal rights say that this vision is really the sinister "hidden agenda" of the animal rights movement. They say that millions of people have been fooled into donating money or otherwise supporting the cause of animal rights without knowing what its real aims are.

It is true that when some of the more radical organizations like PETA or Friends of Animals send out appeals for donations or organize demonstrations, they emphasize their more broadly acceptable aims. As was pointed out when Ingrid Newkirk, one of the founders of PETA, wrote a children's book on animal rights, she never mentioned that she would be opposed to using animals in laboratory testing, even to develop an AIDS vaccine. A lot of dog and cat owners who had once been sympathetic to PETA turned away when they discovered that the organization not only wanted to end abusive treatment of dogs and cats but wanted to get rid of pets altogether.

Still it is not right to charge the animal rights leaders with having a "hidden agenda" or a "secret plan." These leaders have done what the leaders of every other movement have always done; they have put their most popular ideas out front in order to attract the broadest possible support. Once a person is involved in some popular cause, like demonstrating against the slaughter of dolphins, they might then step-by-step move on to accepting basic changes in their outlook. A person might, for example, become a vegetarian.

While leaders of the animal rights movement may not advertise their more extreme views, they make no secret of them either. In books, articles, and interviews many of these leaders have quite freely advocated just the sort of world described in the first paragraph of this chapter. In fact, they are a lot more candid and open about what they believe than the leaders of most political and religious movements.

Another charge brought against the animal rights movement is that those involved support illegal and even terrorist activities. Again the charge is exaggerated. Leaders in the animal rights movement quite openly have supported some kinds of illegal activities, such as breaking into some laboratories to "liberate" animals or to obtain information. But they point out that other "rights" movements throughout history have from time to time advocated breaking the law to serve the cause. Most specifically they point to the activities of environmental groups like Greenpeace. There is nothing secret about support for this kind of lawbreaking, and it probably has wide support even among those who would never think of disobeying the law themselves.

Terrorism, acts that deliberately seek to injure or kill others, is quite different. Any movement that unleashes strong passions, and the animal rights movement certainly does that, can push some people over the edge. The animal rights movement has inspired surprisingly little serious violence of this type. And there is no evidence that leaders of the movement have secretly supported real terrorist acts.

It is also important to repeat, once again, that not all of the groups or individuals who are lumped together under the heading "the animal rights move-

There are many animal rights groups in the
United States right now, each of which has its
own approach to the thorny problems that arise
as one considers the rights of animals versus
those of humans.

ment" share the radical philosophy of an organization like PETA.

So whatever one may think of the objectives of the animal rights movement, it is not made up of a bunch of lying, bomb-throwing loonies.

But how realistic is this vision of a world in which animals are not exploited in any way? The answer has to be, not very realistic at all. It is relatively easy for middle-class American city dwellers to avoid eating meat, wearing leather shoes, and going to the rodeo.

Now look at a nation like India where the majority of the people are by ancient religious tradition vegetarians who revere all life.

They would not use leather, except perhaps from a cow that has died a natural death, and would regard a rodeo as a barbaric activity. Is India a sort of new Eden for the animals? It is not. In this desperately poor and overcrowded nation, wild animals are being squeezed out of existence. Their habitats are being destroyed, not by greedy hotel developers but by poor peasants who need the land to support themselves and their families. On the farms the cows that help plow the land and do other heavy tasks are even more overworked and underfed than the overworked and underfed peasant. The peasant can't afford to "liberate" his animals, because then he would surely starve. In the cities people live in the streets surrounded by packs of dogs that are more miserable than they are. It is no Eden, and no one in the animal rights movement would claim that it is.

There are other problems. While it is obvious that we compete with many animals for living space, gobbling up their natural habitats for housing developments and agricultural development, we also compete directly with some animals for food. This is not as obvious to the majority of Americans who live in cities and suburbs, but it is nonetheless true.

Some animal rights publications have run ads for a "cruelty-free" mousetrap. It is a cage in which the mouse is trapped unharmed and can later be released "into the woods where he belongs." It is a nice cozy thought, with Mr. Mouse scurrying happily among the trees and grass he loves, and safely out of our house. However, this picture completely misrepresents how a mouse lives.

The mouse that lives in our house and eats the bread that we keep in our pantry is a house mouse. It does not "belong" in the woods at all. It is a creature that over hundreds of thousands of years has fully adapted to living off what it can steal from human beings. There are genuine field mice that "belong" in the woods and rarely enter our homes except during the famine times of winter. But when released into the woods that house mouse would do one of two things: it would return immediately to the house from which it had been expelled or it would starve.

Mice, rats, and a host of other creatures destroy huge quantities of grain and other vegetarian foods. They are particularly destructive to the food supplies of poorer nations and are kept in check by the liberal use of poisons, which result in a lingering and painful death for the animals that eat them. But it is inconceivable to imagine that farmers would be able to trap the billions upon billions of mice that attack stored grain and then successfully release these hordes in some wooded area where they would live happily ever after. Throughout history there have been famines caused by rodents destroying food supplies.

Some animal rights supporters look upon city rats that live in alleys and sewers as the equivalent of pathetic stray dogs. It appears to be a creature that is forced to live amid human filth and squalor, and would be much better off "in the wild." That is simply untrue. The city rat that eats our garbage is larger, stronger, and healthier than the same sort of rat that lives in the country. Our cities are their "homes." What are we to do about them? Rats not only destroy food, they spread disease. The worst epidemic in human history, the bubonic plague, was spread by the fleas that live on rats.

These are not trivial or unimportant questions. They go to the very heart of the animal rights philosophy.

The most radical of animal rights supporters view *homo sapiens* as just another species, with no more intrinsic rights than a chimpanzee, a house mouse, or a rat, for that matter. However, biologically speaking at least, we are the most successful species on Earth. (The cockroaches might quarrel with that judgment. They have been around a lot longer and despite our best efforts are more numerous than ever. Let us say we are the most successful large species living today.) The human species has been able to adapt to living in every conceivable habitat, from the polar regions to the tropics. No other single species has so wide a distribution. And our numbers are increasing dramatically from year to year. Biologically speaking, a species does not have to be happy or moral to be successful. The only thing necessary for success is that a species "be fruitful and multiply" and we have certainly done that.

A large herd of elephants will strip an area of vegetation and trample the undergrowth into dust, thus robbing many other species of both their food and homes. Yet elephants are strict vegetarians. If we are just another species, then it is unrealistic to expect that we will not behave like all the other species of animals in the history of life on Earth. We will do whatever is necessary for our personal survival and for the continued success of our species. Like the elephant herd we are large, numerous, and have a great impact on our surroundings.

Unrestricted population growth is a disaster, not only for other animals but potentially for the human species as well. Unless we get the human population under control, animal rights will never be more than a fringe issue—something that only the affluent, a tiny portion of the world's human population, have the luxury of worrying about. And right now it seems we are a long way from controlling our own population. In fact, despite some improvements, we are still a long way from recognizing the rights of other members of our own species.

So the real criticism of the animal rights movement is not that its leadership harbors some sort of sinister hidden agenda. Certainly not that it is a terrorist organization or that those who believe in animal rights care nothing for human beings. The philosophers of the movement can construct a compelling case for animal rights, in theory. But the theory has very little connection to the real world. The theory assumes that our large and ever more numerous species can somehow exist without having any real impact on all the other species we come in contact with. And that is unrealistic.

Does that mean that the animal rights movement is a foolish and misguided waste of time—something that can and should be ignored? No!

Animal rights activists have given new life and energy to the old humane and animal welfare movements. The activists have opened a lot of doors and quite literally forced us to look behind them and see what is being done to animals today.

Does the modern world really need the steel leghold trap and the hunting ranch? Are the rodeo and the roadside zoo just good clean family entertainment?

The animal rights movement has had its successes. The wearing of fur is way down, and some particularly painful and unnecessary animal testing has been reduced. There has even been some small progress on better treatment for the animals we raise for food.

Because the animal rights movement won't let us turn away, or comfort ourselves with fantasy tales of the happy chickens and pigs in Farmer Brown's barnyard, it compels us all to make some choices. Perhaps we won't buy that leather coat, perhaps we won't eat as much meat, or eat meat at all.

For all its unreality, for all its strident, obnoxious, misguided, and occasionally even dangerous behavior, the animal rights movement has, on balance, been a very good thing. If it didn't exist, conditions would be even worse for animals. And it appeals to what is best in the human animal.

TWENTY WAYS TO SAVE THE ANIMALS

11

We Americans are great list makers—ten ways to lose weight, fifty ways to save the Earth—that sort of thing. We like our solutions neat, quick, and easy—especially easy. But as we have seen, animal rights is not an easy subject. The animal rights movement has raised issues for which there are no neat, quick, and easy answers, perhaps no real answers at all. That does not mean we have an excuse to throw up our hands, or more accurately, put our hands over our eyes, and say there is nothing that one person can do, so why bother. Throughout this book there have been practical suggestions about what you can do, right now. This is the place to repeat some of these suggestions.

1.   Become a vegetarian. That suggestion would probably be at the top of any animal rights activist's list. It's a perfectly healthy life-style, and it's a lot easier to be a vegetarian today than it was just a few

years ago. But it's still a big step, and easier is not the same as easy. You don't have to be a purist. Just resolve to eat less meat. You may even gradually become a vegetarian.

2. Avoid certain kinds of meat, like veal, where the animals are treated with exceptional cruelty.

3. Try to have your family buy free-range meats and organic eggs if these are available.

4. Buy as many cruelty-free products as possible. Following this chapter is a list of places where you can get more information about products developed without animal testing.

5. Don't dissect animals in the classroom or use animals as part of an experiment for a science fair. You don't need to cut up a frog to learn biology; there are plenty of alternatives. Today schools are more sensitive to the opinions of those students who don't want to dissect.

6. Don't hunt, and if your family owns land in the country make sure that there are plenty of POSTED—NO HUNTING signs nailed to the trees. The signs won't always keep hunters off your property, but they help.

7. Openly and actively oppose any local events like "pigeon shoots" where the central activity is killing or otherwise abusing animals for fun. There can be absolutely no excuse for the continued existence of such events in modern America. Negative publicity will not only help to bring such festivals of cruelty to an end, it will also help raise public awareness on the entire range of animal rights issues.

8.   Don't wear fur. Fur trapping and ranching are exceptionally cruel, and no one needs fur to keep warm today. This is an area where the animal rights movement has had a great impact, and there is a real possibility that the wearing of fur will become as much of an anachronism as the wearing of powdered wigs.

9.   Don't wear leather. Most leather comes from animals that have already been slaughtered for meat, so avoiding that leather jacket probably isn't going to save the lives of any animals. But the symbolism is important. Not wearing leather makes a statement.

10.   Make sure your dog and cat are spayed or neutered. The fate of millions of unwanted animals is tragic—don't contribute to the problem.

11.   Don't *ever* buy a dog, cat, exotic bird, or any wild animal like a ferret in a pet shop. The dogs usually come from puppy mills, heaven knows where the cats come from, the birds are trapped and shipped under horrible conditions, and wild animals don't make good pets and don't usually survive for very long. And don't buy any pet products in shops that sell these animals. If people stop patronizing these shops, they'll get the message.

12.   If you want a dog or cat, seriously consider getting one from a shelter. These animals need you and will return the love you give them tenfold.

13.   If you really want a purebred dog go to a breeder and check out the kennel. If the breeder is a good one, he or she should be checking you out as well, not just trying to sell you a dog.

14. If you see an animal being abused, starved, beaten, or tied out day and night in all kinds of weather, report this to your local humane society. Animal abuse and neglect are against the law. Although these laws are often not very vigorously enforced, a complaint can stimulate action.

15. Don't go to the rodeo, the circus, or any other form of "entertainment" that is based on cruelty to and exploitation of animals. Since rodeos and small circuses are often sponsored by local organizations, letters to the organization or the newspapers can often be very effective in stopping such displays.

16. Before you go to any zoo make sure it is a member of the American Association of Zoological Parks and Aquariums (AAZPA), a national organization that sets minimal standards of treatment for zoo animals. Zoos that are members usually post this information near the entrance. Most large zoos are members; most small "roadside zoos" are not. Member zoos are often far from perfect, but they are trying. If your school plans a class trip to a zoo have your teacher check out its AAZPA membership.

17. Saving forests, wetlands, and other natural areas is a way of saving animals. Anything you can do for the environment, from recycling plastics to saving energy, is going to help the animals. When the environment is destroyed it is the animals that suffer first.

18. Read up on animal rights issues. There is lots of information and lots of controversy on this subject. If animals are important to you, you owe it to yourself

to be knowledgeable. A good place to start is with the list of books on pages 121–22.

19. There are loads of organizations that will provide you with information on how to become actively involved in various animal rights activities. These organizations range from the very moderate to the very radical. A list of the more prominent animal rights groups is on pages 118–20.

20. Be an example. Improvements in the lives of animals come only when human attitudes change. And attitudes, even deep-seated ones, can and do change. An obvious example is that fur coats are no longer popular. The most potent force in the world for changing attitudes is not a book or a video but a personal contact. Talk to your friends, your parents, and other relatives. Tell them what you know and what you feel. One person can make a difference. *You* can make a difference.

CRUELTY-FREE PRODUCTS

If your doctor gives you a prescription you will probably never know if the medicine was developed through the use of animal tests. But with cosmetics and many cleaners there now are companies that specialize in producing products developed without animal testing. They are all perfectly safe, although some may be more expensive. Write or call the following for their lists of cruelty-free products.

Beauty Without Cruelty USA. 175 West 12th Street, Suite 15G, New York, NY 10128-8725. (212) 989-8073.

The Body Shop. Hanover Technical Center, 45 Horsehill Road, Cedar Knolls, NJ 07927-2003. (201) 984-9200.

Ecco Bella. 125 Pompton Plains Crossroad, Wayne, NJ 07470. (201) 890-7077.

John Paul Mitchell Systems. P.O. Box 10597, Beverly Hills, CA 90213.

Shoppers Guide to Cruelty-Free Products. P.O. Box 22505, Sacramento, CA 95822.

Tom's of Maine. Railroad Avenue, Kennebunk, ME 04042.

ORGANIZATIONS

There are scores of organizations that are involved in the animal rights movement. Some are regional or local, others are concerned with a specific issue, like the treatment of animals in entertainment, or a particular animal, like the dolphin or the elephant. A large number of environmental groups might be classed as animal rights groups. There are also plenty of groups that are on the other side of at least some parts of the animal rights debate. What follows is a list of some of the more prominent groups, particularly those that were mentioned in this book. To repeat, one more time, although all the organizations on this list say they work for better treatment of animals, they may differ sharply on specifics. For example, the ASPCA says that experimentation on animals "should be permitted only where there are no known feasible alternatives." PETA, on the other hand, opposes experimentation on animals under any circumstances. Some organizations actively oppose particular aspects of the animal rights agenda. The AKC rejects the animal rights campaign against purebred dogs, for example. And one organization, NAIA, finds the entire animal rights movement dangerous.

Alliance for Animals. P.O. Box 909, Boston, MA 02103. (617) 265-7577. An active volunteer organization involved in a variety of animal causes, particularly in the New England area.

American Association of Zoological Parks and Aquariums (AAZPA). 7970-D Old Georgetown Road, Bethesda, MD 20814-2493. (301) 907-7777. All the major zoos and aquariums belong to this organization.

American Humane Association. 63 Inverness Drive East, Englewood, CO 80112. (303) 792-9900. This organization is involved in training those who work in animal shelters and in getting animal protection legislation passed.

The American Kennel Club (AKC). 51 Madison Avenue, New York, NY 10010. (212) 696-8200. The official purebred dog organization.

American Society for the Prevention of Cruelty to Animals (ASPCA). 424 E. 92nd Street, New York, NY 10128. (212) 876-7700. The oldest and largest of the American animal welfare organizations.

Animal Welfare Institute. P.O. Box 3650, Washington, D.C. 20007. (202) 337-2333. A middle-of-the-road animal welfare organization and an excellent source of publications for classroom use.

Defenders of Wildlife. 1244 19th Street N.W., Washington, D.C. 20036. (202) 659-9510. An organization concerned primarily with wild animals.

Farm Animal Reform Movement (FARM). P.O. Box 30654, Bethesda, MD 20824. (301) 530-1737. A vegetarian group formed to expose the cruelties of factory farming and to initiate direct action projects.

Friends of Animals. P.O. Box 1244, Norwalk, CT 06856. (203) 866-5223. One of the more radical and active animal rights groups.

Greyhound Friends, Inc. Louise Coleman, 167 Saddle Hill Road, Hopkinton, MA 01748. (508) 435-5969. If you want to adopt a retired racing greyhound this is the place to contact.

International Network for Religion and Animals (INRA). P.O. Box 1335, North Wales, PA 19454-0335. (215) 721-1908. This group holds that all the world's major religions preach that animals should be treated with compassion and respect.

National Animal Interest Alliance (NAIA). P.O. Box 66579, Portland, OR 97290-6579. (503) 761-8962. A small organization that supports kindness to animals but strongly opposes the animal rights movement.

National Anti-Vivisection Society. 53 West Jackson Boulevard, Chicago, IL 60604. (312) 427-6065. An organization specifically opposed to the use of animals in research.

People for the Ethical Treatment of Animals (PETA). P.O. Box 42516, Washington, D.C. 20015. (301) 770-7444. The most active, outspoken, radical, and controversial of all the large animal rights groups.

BOOKS AND PUBLICATIONS

Over the past twenty years there has been a flood of books related to animal rights. Listed below are some of the more significant. Those marked with an asterisk are aimed at younger readers.

* *The Animal Rights Handbook.* Venice, Calif.: The Living Planet Press, 1990. Written for the ASPCA, this little volume contains everything from a list of companies that make cruelty-free products to advice on how to write your congressional representative on animal rights issues. It's very useful.

Amory, Cleveland. *Man Kind?* New York: Dell, 1980. A furious indictment of the way humans treat animals by one of America's most popular writers and best-known animal activists.

Budiansky, Stephen. *The Covenant of the Wild: Why Animals Chose Domestication.* New York: Morrow, 1992. This author argues that humans have not really exploited domestic animals.

Harrison, Ruth. *Animal Machines.* London: Vincent Stuart, 1964. The opening shot in the war against factory farming.

* Koebner, Linda. *For Kids Who Love Animals*. Venice, Calif.: The Living Planet Press, 1991. This book, prepared for the ASPCA, offers solid information and good advice.

* Newkirk, Ingrid. *Kids Can Save the Animals*. New York: Time-Warner, 1991. Practical advice, but a bit cutesy. By the national director of PETA.

Pringle, Laurence. *The Animal Rights Controversy*. New York: Harcourt, 1989. An overview of the conflict between the animal rights movement and the research and farming industries.

Regan, Tom. *The Case for Animal Rights*. Berkeley, Calif.: University of California Press, 1983. The most complete philosophical discussion of animal rights.

Rifkin, Jeremy. *Beyond Beef: The Rise and Fall of the Cattle Industry*. New York: Dutton, 1991. This alarming book argues that the cattle industry not only exploits animals but is a threat to humans as well.

Robbins, John. *Diet for a New America*. Walpole, N.H.: Stillpoint Publishing, 1987. A stinging indictment of the meat and dairy industries and a plea for a vegetarian life-style.

Singer, Peter. *Animal Liberation*, rev. ed. New York: Random House, 1990. This book is the "bible" of the animal rights movement.

———— (ed.). *In Defense of Animals*. New York: Basil Blackwell Inc., 1985. A collection of essays on the animal rights movement by some of its leaders.

Many of the organizations have their own regular magazines and newsletters. Here are a few others.

The Animals' Agenda, P.O. Box 6809, Syracuse, NY 13217.
Animals Magazine, 350 Huntington Avenue, Boston, MA 02130.
The Animals' Voice, P.O. Box 341-347, Los Angeles, CA 90034.
Between the Species, P.O. Box 254, Berkeley, CA 94701.

NOTES

Chapter One

The biblical quotes are from Genesis 1:27–30 and Genesis 9:1–4.

One of the angriest denunciations of the animal rights movement was written by Patti Strand, president of the National Animal Interest Alliance, for the dog breeders magazine *Dog Watch*, December 13, 1991.

Chapter Two

Practically all books on animal rights contain a great deal of information on the cruelties of modern farming. One of the best and most fact-filled brief summations of the case is Jim Mason's article "Brave New Farm," which appears in the book *In Defense of Animals*, edited by Peter Singer and published in 1985.

The statistics on the damage inflicted by cattle grazing come from Jeremy Rifkin's 1991 book *Beyond Beef: The Rise and Fall of the Cattle Industry*.

Chapter 3

Peter Singer reviewed the case of Fran Trutt and the British letter bombs in the new preface to the second edition of *Animal Liberation*, published in 1990.

Tom Regan's quote will be found on page 393 of his *The Case for Animal Rights*, published in 1983.

More information on the legal status of students who don't wish to participate in biology class dissections is on page 69 of *The Animal Rights Handbook*, prepared for the ASPCA.

The book in which Ingrid Newkirk failed to mention AIDS is *Kids Can Save the Animals*, published in 1991.

Chapter 4

Information on the white-tailed deer can be found in "The Most Dangerous Animal" by Richard Borders, published in the *New York Times Magazine*, June 13, 1991.

Philip Windeatt's quotes from his article "They Clearly Now See the Link: Militant Voices," printed in Singer's *In Defense of Animals*.

Information on the prices charged by hunting ranches is in "Exposing the Zoo-Hunting Ranch Connection" by Lisa A. Landres in *Act'ion Line*, November/December 1991. This is a publication of the group Friends of Animals.

Chapter 5

The trappers present their position in an article in the *New York Times*, February 9, 1992, page 45.

A brief history of the anti-fur movement can be found in *The Animal Rights Handbook*, page 11.

In *How Kids Can Save the Animals*, pages 142–145, Ingrid Newkirk outlines the most extreme animal rights position, which disapproves of wearing wool and silk as well as fur and leather.

Chapter 6

A comprehensive explanation of the views of more radical members of the animal rights movement on pet overpopulation and pet ownership in general is found in a special August 1991 edition of *Paws News*, a publication of the Progressive Animal Welfare Society.

Information on the bulldog—indeed on all purebred dogs everywhere in the world—is in the massive *Atlas of Dog Breeds of the World* by Bonnie Wilcox, D.V.M., and Chris Walkowicz, THF Publications, 1989.

The animal rights side of the San Mateo County ordinance controversy is covered fully in *The Fund for Animals Instruction Manual*, which also provides information on having similar ordinances introduced in other parts of the country. The response of dog and cat breeders can be found in almost every issue of such publications as *The AKC Gazette, Dog World*, and *Cats Magazine* from 1990 to 1992.

Chapter 7

Practically every animal rights and human organization has published literature on the abuses of rodeos and circuses. A good and accessible summary appears on page 95 of the ASPCA's *For Kids Who Love Animals*.

An article on legal cockfighting appeared on the front page of the *Wall Street Journal*, March 18, 1992.

Chapter 8

The controversy surrounding the odyssey of Timmy the gorilla was covered extensively in local media in both Cleveland and New York in late 1991 and early 1992. The stories were invariably cloyingly cute and coy. More accurate information on the need for the captive breeding of gorillas was supplied by the Bronx Zoo.

Ingrid Newkirk's quote on animals staying "in their homes" appears on page 120 of *Kids Can Save the Animals*. The preface of that book has a graphic explanation of the philosophy behind this statement.

Information that some animals from the San Diego Zoo had been sold to hunting ranches first became known to the general public in a *60 Minutes* broadcast in 1990. Additional information appeared in Lisa A. Landres's article in the November/December 1991 issue of *Act'ion Line*, published by Friends of Animals.

A good, short (and pro-zoo) article on the controversy is "Just Too Beastly for Words" by Jesse Birnbaum, *Time*, June 24, 1991, page 60.

Chapter 9

Information on the Round Island controversy and a good overall look at the problems that animal rights present for conservationists is "Animal Rights: A Growing Moral Dilemma" by F. Wayne King, *Animal Kingdom*, January/February, 1988.

Chapter 10

The angriest arguments against the animal rights movement can be found in Patti Strand's article, cited in Chapter One.

Ingrid Newkirk's advice on how to get rid of a mouse in your house is on page 126 of *Kids Can Save the Animals*.

An update on the animal rights controversy, particularly how it affects students and schools, appears in the *Wall Street Journal*, September 2, 1992, page B1.

INDEX